SCROLL SAW BENCH GUIDE

SCROLL SAW BENCH GUIDE

Zachary Taylor

STERLING PUBLISHING CO. INC., NEW YORK

10 9 8 7 6 5 4 3 2 1

Series Editor: Michael Cea
Series Designer: Chris Swirnoff

Published 2002 by Sterling Publishing Company, Inc.
387 Park Avenue South, New York, New York 10016
Originally published under the title *Scroll Saw: Workshop Bench reference*
© 1999 by Zachary Taylor
Distributed in Canada by Sterling Publishing
c/o Canadian Manda Group, One Atlantic Avenue, Suite 105
Toronto, Ontario, Canada M6K 3E7
Distributed in Great Britain and Europe by Cassell PLC
Wellington House, 125 Strand, London WC2R 0BB, England
Distributed in Australia by Capricorn Link (Australia) Pty. Ltd.
P.O. Box 704, Windsor, NSW 2756 Australia
Printed in China
All rights reserved

Sterling ISBN 0-8069-9139-9

Dedication

To Douglas Woodward,

a fine engineer

whose legendary design skills

have made such

valuable contributions

to the scroll saw

Acknowledgments

The author extends his grateful thanks to the following people, who, in one way or another, contributed to this book:

Colin Bullock and Christopher Isotta, for help with
the word-processing

Roger Buse of Hegner *(United Kingdom)*

Terry Davies of Poolewood *(United Kingdom)*

Nick Davidson of Craft Supplies, Ltd. *(United Kingdom)*

David Fisher, for his drawings

Trudy Hoepffner of Hegner *(Germany)*

Daniel V. Holman of Adjustable Clamp Co. *(United States)*

Mark J. Schwatz of Penn State Industries *(United States)*

Brothers Shah of Kenton Photographic Colour Laboratories, Ltd.
    (United Kingdom)

Alex Snodgrass of PS Wood *(United States)*

Roger Stanton of Rexon, Ltd. *(United Kingdom)*

Glen Tizzard of Draper Tools, Ltd. *(United Kingdom)*

Douglas Woodward, manufacturer of Diamond Scroll Saws
    (United Kingdom)

Malcolm Woodward of Micro-Flame, Ltd., Dremel Machines
    (United Kingdom and United States)

Contents

Introduction 11

CHAPTER 1

Scroll-Saw Components and Features 13

Types of Scroll Saw 13
    C-Frame Scroll Saw 13
    Parallel-Arm Scroll Saw 13
    Comparing Parallel and C-Frame
        Scroll Saws 18
    Bench or Floor Models? 21

Standard Features of the Scroll Saw 21
    Features to Consider in a Scroll Saw 21
    Stroke Speed and Depth 22
    Switches 22
    Blade-Tensioning Devices 26
    Blade-Tensioning Guidelines 27
    Worktable Tilt 28
    Dust Blower 29
    Hold-Down 30
    Guards 32
    Storage Box 33
    Blade-Breakage Device 33
    Rubber Feet 34
    Table Inserts 34

Maintaining Scroll-Saw Components 35

CHAPTER 2

Accessories 39

Miscellaneous Optional Accessories 39
    Foot Switch 39

Dust-Extraction Unit 40
Flexible Shaft 41
Hold-Downs 42
Accessories for Abrading Wood 45
Machine Stand 47
Magnifier 47
Vibration Absorption Mat 48
Accessory for Cutting Thin Wood or Metal 49
Coolant Dispenser 51
Blade Container 51
Geometrical Protractor 53
Awls for Hole-Boring 53

Jigs 56
    Straight Fence 56
    Finger Fence 59
    Circle-Cutting Jig 61
    Ancillary Table 63

CHAPTER 3

Saw Blades 67

Blade-Selection Guidelines 67

Basic Blade Information 71

Blade Types 73
    Standard Wood-Cutting Blades 73
    Metal-Cutting Blades 74
    Skip-Tooth Blades 74
    Reverse-Tooth Blades 75
    Spiral Blades 75
    Abrasive-Coated Rods 76

Improving Blades 76
    Rounding Blade Backs 76

Removing Burrs   77
Modifying the Cross-Pins on Pin-End
    Blades   77
Modifying the Widths of Pin-End Blades   77
Cutting Workpieces Longer than the
    Throat Depth   77
Blade Holders   78
Blade-Holding System Guidelines   78
Adjustments and Tracking Procedures   91
Right-Angle Blade Adjustment   91
Setting Blade Angles Other Than 90
    Degrees   92
Adjusting for Longer Blades   94
Straight Tracking   94

CHAPTER 4

**Basic Sawing Principles
and Techniques   97**

Blades, Stroke Speed, and Feed Rate   97

Hand Placement   98
Correct Hand Technique   100

Steering Techniques   101
What About the Saw Line?   101
Dealing With Blade Bias   102
One-The-Spot Turns   102
Making On-The-Spot Turns with Various
    Blades   103

CHAPTER 5

**Sawing Wood and Non-Wood
Materials   105**

Cutting Wood   105

Cutting Metal   107

Cutting Plastics   108

Cutting Ivory, Bone and Imitations   109
Cutting Ceramics, Glass, and Stones   110

CHAPTER 6

Cutting Techniques   111

Crosscutting   111

Rip-Cutting   112

Cutting Curves   113

Cutting Circles   114

Cutting Large Workpieces   116

Cutting Small Workpieces   118

Making Templates for Curved Shapes   120

Internal-Sawing   124

Marquetry   126
Boulle Method of Stack-Cutting Veneer   126
"Flawless" Marquetry   128

Intarsia   130
Intarsia with Wedge Inlays   130
Hollow-Form Intarsia   134

Sawing with a Spiral Blade   137

CHAPTER 7

Patterns   141

Copying and Transferring Patterns   141

Applying the Pattern to the Wood   143

Using Templates As Patterns   143

CHAPTER 8

Safety Procedures   145

Glossary   149

Metric Equivalents Chart   153

Index   155

Introduction

Most people prompted to open this book are probably acquainted in some way with scroll saws. For those who are already advanced scroll-sawyers, the information will hopefully encourage even greater efforts to produce what one of my American friends calls a "gee-whiz" project. There is help here for the self-taught who have already fumbled their way from those clumsy first attempts to some acceptable level of craftsmanship, but who are wondering how to get more out of their scroll saw. And beginners can treat the following information as one would the information in a textbook, reading the pages from beginning to end because they provide essential basic information on scroll-saw use, including guidance on determining which scroll saw is best suited for their needs.

As its title implies, this book is best used as a workshop companion. It is designed so that the scroll-saw user will have handy access to essential information. However, it will be helpful to all scroll-sawyers, no matter how they use it. I applaud those who read this introduction before thumbing through the book for a quick look at its contents. They are most likely the type who enjoy a fresh start, ignoring no dark corner in the search for information. Pedantic plodders are also welcome. But this book will prove especially appealing to those seeking an instant "fix" for a special woodworking problem, who can then simply turn to the appropriate section.

The scroll saw, also sometimes referred to as a fretsaw or jigsaw, has evolved from a hand-driven frame saw whose application required manual dexterity and lots of time, to a motor-driven power tool capable of achieving great cutting precision. Some may feel that it should be used exclusively for ornamentation or decoration, and while it is ideally suited to the creation of elegant masterpieces of, for example, marquetry, it is not limited to this pursuit. Hobbyists and craftsmen at every level from beginner to professional, as well as serious mass-producers in industrial settings, rely on the scroll saw. It is equally helpful in a multitude of general woodworking tasks such as cutting small pieces and joints and, when used with the correct saw blade, can saw many materials in addition to wood, such as fiberboard, metals, and plastics. All these tasks, as well as the proper selection of the correct saw blade, are covered in the following pages.

Potential users may shrink instinctively from the scroll saw, as they might from other power saws, anticipating danger from the blade. Unlike its larger and more powerful relatives, however, the scroll saw is the safest type of machine.

Zachary Taylor at work on a project.

Band saws and circular saws have the unfortunate characteristic of drawing the workpiece or fingers into the blade. Scroll-saw blades, due to their reciprocating action, have the tendency to pull away on the upstroke, and these blades are so comparatively small with such fine teeth that an accident may produce a superficial nick rather than a permanent maiming. Techniques applied correctly should prevent accidents of this sort. That is why it is so important that you read Chapter 8 to become familiar with proper safety procedures.

The information set out herein is based on my experience as a long-time exponent of the scroll saw in my professions as an instrument-maker, a woodworking author, and teacher. It contains the latest information on scroll saws that can be found on both sides of the Atlantic, including recent improvements in their designs and an examination of the most helpful accessories.

My experience with scroll saws harkens back to my ninth birthday, when my father gave me a "hobby" hand fretsaw. I grew up using that saw and have worked with the motorized versions ever since. Occasionally, I still use the "hobby" fretsaw to produce by hand an extra-special creation such as a lute rose.

No projects are given in this book. Instead, I have concentrated on providing detailed instructions and illustrations that will develop skills essential for releasing the potential of this versatile machine. So whether you are someone with absolutely no idea of how to use a scroll saw or a professional looking to quickly resolve a woodworking problem, keep this book by the scroll saw as a handy companion.

Zachary Taylor

1 Scroll-Saw Components and Features

Types of Scroll Saw

Anyone who switches on a motorized scroll saw for the first time will probably understand at a glance what it is supposed to do: make many types of saw cuts, primarily in wood. Developed from a simple, hand-held, manually operated tool used several hundred years ago, it can perform sawing operations that no other machine saw can. The component most responsible for the effectiveness of the scroll saw is the saw blade, which is held between the ends of upper and lower arms, reciprocating vertically through a hole in the worktable.

Two major types of scroll saw are available, excluding models that fall into specialized categories (such as the fixed-arm machines incorporating spring-return mechanisms that are becoming outdated). These are C-frame and parallel-arm saws. The major distinction between these two types of saw is in the motion of the frame, or arms. C-frame and parallel-arm scroll saws do fundamentally the same kind of work. However, they operate differently, so the resulting work from each respective machine will have some disparity. To understand this, it is necessary to examine both machines.

C-FRAME SCROLL SAW

A C-frame scroll saw has an open-ended frame that resembles an elongated letter C (1-1). The frame pivots near its rear, permitting it to swing up and down vertically (1-2 to 1-5). The ends of the saw blade are attached by blade holders fixed to the top and bottom terminals at the open ends of the frame. A worktable, with a central hole through which the saw blade passes, is held within, but separate from, the frame. The worktable is normally oriented at right angles to the saw blade, but this angle may be changed to permit bevel-sawing. The vertical motion that creates the sawing action is achieved by an electric motor. A mechanical device converts the circular motion of the motor spindle to the reciprocation of the frame. Tension on the saw blade is produced by an apparatus that usually incorporates a screw thread (1-6 to 1-8). Since the frame is a one-piece unit that swings on one pivot, it follows that the path of the sawblade is not perfectly vertical, but instead is part of an arc.

PARALLEL-ARM SCROLL SAW

Unlike the C-frame scroll saw, the parallel-arm scroll saw has two separate arms (1-9). The arms are

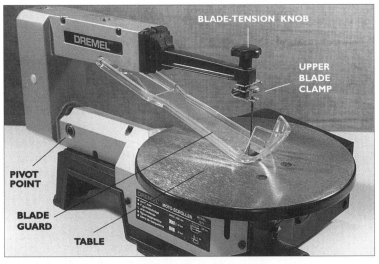

BLADE-TENSION KNOB

UPPER BLADE CLAMP

PIVOT POINT

BLADE GUARD

TABLE

1-1. A basic C-frame scroll saw with a single-speed motor, a tilting table, and guard/hold-down.

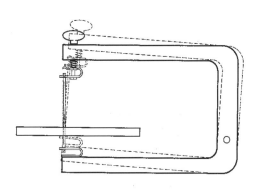

1-2. How the frame on a C-frame scroll saw pivots.

1-3. A one-piece casting forms the C-frame of this scroll saw, seen with half its cover removed. The frame's reciprocating action is similar to that of a parallel-arm saw with a Pitman-arm connected to the motor shaft, as shown in 1-9.

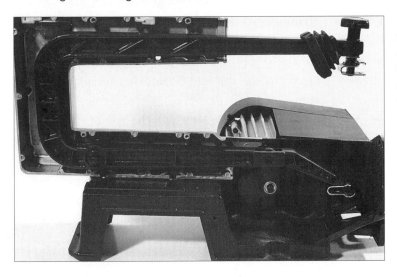

1-4 (below left). The frame design on this C-frame scroll saw is somewhat different from that of the C-frame scroll saw shown in 1-3. The upper arm is hinged for applying blade tension. *1-5 (below right).* A close-up of the Pitman arm that connects the lower frame with the motor shaft. The lower frame and the motor shaft are at right angles to each other.

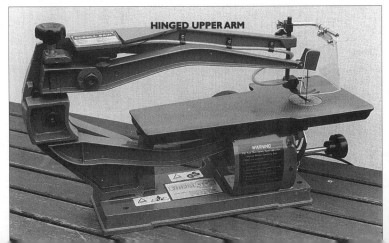

HINGED UPPER ARM

PRODUCING TENSION ON A C-FRAME SAW BLADE

1-6. *The hinging arrangement of a C-frame scroll saw. At the top of the assembly is the hand knob used for blade-tension adjustment. The nut on the upper arm is attached to the pivot, allowing the upper arm to be adjusted at different angles. In the lower cavity is the main frame pivot on which the C-shaped frame reciprocates.*

1-7. *An opposite view of the hinging arrangement shown in 1-6. This view shows the two socket screws attached to the main pillar of the ancillary arm that carries the guard/hold-down.*

1-8. *A lift-up guard can be raised for access to the blade and blade holder. It is attached to the height-adjusting device that also houses the dust-blower nozzle.*

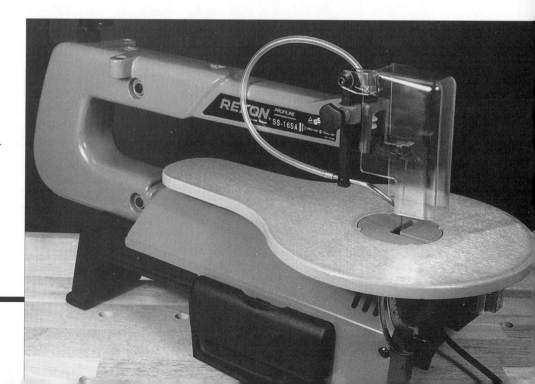

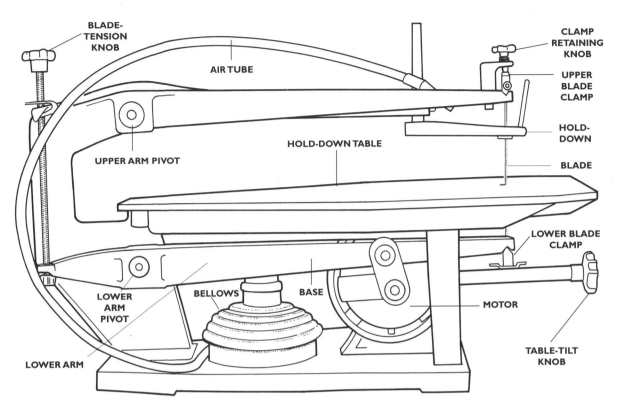

BLADE-
TENSION
KNOB

AIR TUBE

CLAMP
RETAINING
KNOB

UPPER
BLADE
CLAMP

HOLD-
DOWN

BLADE

UPPER ARM PIVOT

HOLD-DOWN TABLE

LOWER BLADE
CLAMP

LOWER
ARM
PIVOT

BELLOWS

BASE

MOTOR

LOWER ARM

TABLE-TILT
KNOB

1-9. *A view of the parts of a parallel-arm scroll saw.*

1-10. *A typical high-quality parallel-arm scroll saw with a variable-speed motor, a tilting table, a dust blower, and a provision for a guard/hold-down device.*

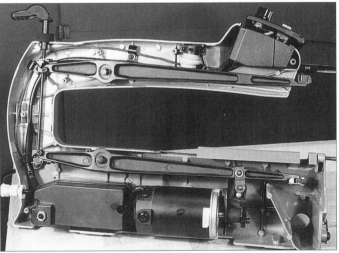

1-11. *The side cover on this parallel-arm scroll saw has been removed, revealing the upper and lower arms. Notice the pivots, one above the other where the arms are broadest, and the connecting rod at the rear terminals of the arms. As the motor revolves, the circular motion is converted to reciprocation by a Pitman-arm connection. In this model, the motor spindle is arranged in line with the arms, which allows the table to tilt to the left or the right.*

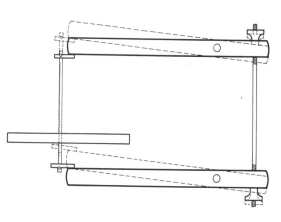

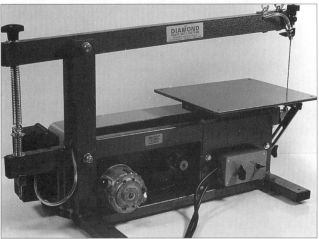

1-12 (top left). A Pitman-arm connection on a parallel-arm scroll saw. As with the example in 1-11, the motor is in line with the arm, allowing the table to incline to the left and right, an unusual facility. *1-13 (top right).* How the frame pivots on a parallel-arm scroll saw. *1-14 (above left).* With the worktable removed, the lower arm and the motor are visible on this parallel-arm scroll saw. The connecting rod between the arms is spring-activated, which raises the upper arm if the blade breaks. This prevents damage to the workpiece or the operator. *1-15 (above right).* With the cover removed the sophisticated gear train and counterbalancing system is revealed. At the rear is an independently powered air pump that gives a constant-pressure air flow.

---

of equal length, pivoted at identical points arranged vertically, one above the other (1-10 to 1-12). When the rear ends of the arms are drawn closer together by a screw mechanism, opposite movement occurs on the other side of the pivots, widening the gap between the front of the arms. This applies tension to the saw blade that is attached to the front terminals of the arms (1-13).

If the distance between the rear and front terminals is equal, it follows as a geometrical property that the arms when activated must remain parallel to each other. The work-tables on parallel-arm scroll saws are fitted in a similar way to those on C-frame scroll saws, and the circular-to-reciprocating motion achieved by the same mechanical principles (1-14 and 1-15).

Text continues on page 21

COMPARING PARALLEL AND C-FRAME SCROLL SAWS

Let's compare the cutting actions of parallel- and C-frame scroll saws. We'll use as an example scroll saws that have a 20-inch throat, a 1-inch stroke, and which are fitted with a 5-inch blade. In the case of the C-frame scroll saw, if the pivot is at the rear end of the frame and level with the table, then the upstroke would withdraw the blade from the workface by approximately 3 degrees, or about .025 inch between the blade and the top of a 1-inch work-face. Parallel-arm scroll saws would withdraw the blade from the workface by a similar amount, but they would do so while maintaining a vertical motion (1-16 - 1-19).

Whether or not it is desirable to have the saw blade reciprocating vertically rather than with a slight backswing is dependent on the type of work to be undertaken. If, for example, mostly straight lines or gentle curves are to be cut, a C-frame scroll saw will perform as well as, and, in fact, more aggressively than a parallel-arm saw. The latter is more efficient for the navigation of tight curves or smaller radii and, in general, leaves a better finish in the process. It is possible to work on small radii with a C-frame scroll saw provided the workpiece is relatively thin; otherwise, if thicker material is being cut, there is more strain on the blade, and also the finish suffers. Most manufacturers are currently producing parallel-arm machines due to popular demand, although the cheaper end of the market still contains a small selection of C-frame models. As with all machines, no matter what the quality, its performance may be improved or impaired by the operator.

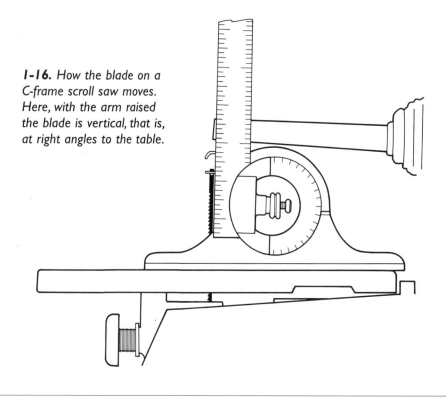

1-16. How the blade on a C-frame scroll saw moves. Here, with the arm raised the blade is vertical, that is, at right angles to the table.

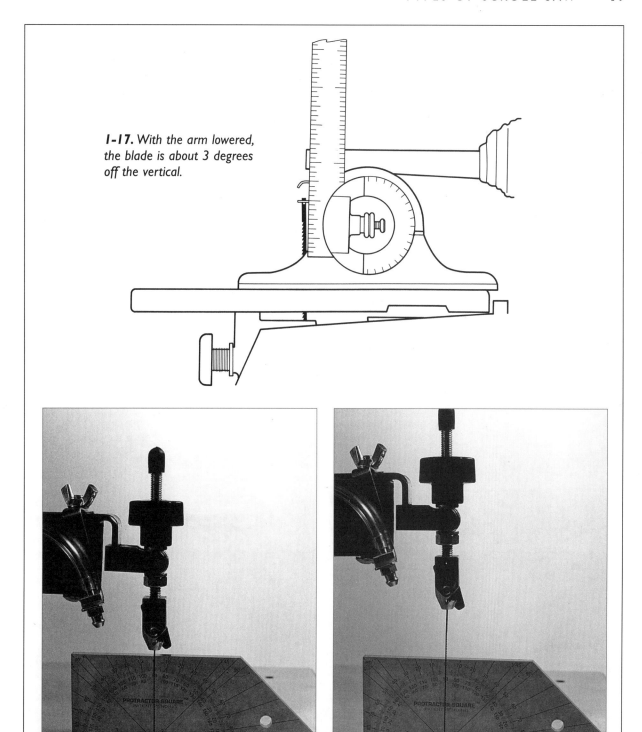

1-17. *With the arm lowered, the blade is about 3 degrees off the vertical.*

1-18 and 1-19. *In the case of this parallel-arm saw, when the blade is measured at its lowest (left) and highest (right) positions, it is clear that it remains perpendicular to the table.*

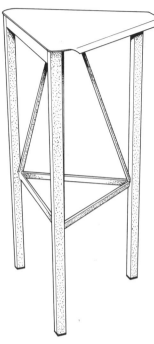

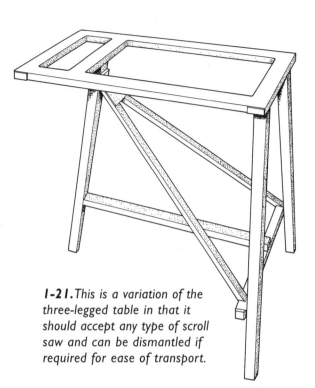

1-20. A sturdy three-legged table to which a scroll saw can be bolted or clamped. In keeping with the principle of the tripod, it remains steady even if the ground is uneven. Refer to Bench or Floor Models? on page 21 for a discussion of the advantages and disadvantages of using bench or floor-model scroll saws.

1-21. This is a variation of the three-legged table in that it should accept any type of scroll saw and can be dismantled if required for ease of transport.

1-22. This set-up is ideal for the serious sawyer. The stand is fitted with a scroll saw, and a swivel chair that can be adjusted for height is nearby. A foot switch is attached to the stand, off the floor, for safety.

1-23. The scroll saw and stand shown in 1-22 being operated from a standing position.

Providing that the saw-blade length is correct as specified for the machine, the parallel arms should cut in a perfectly vertical motion. In fact, due to the lifting of the arms on the return stroke, the blade is drawn back from the sawn face very slightly, relieving pressure at the workface. These details will be examined in the following section.

BENCH OR FLOOR MODELS?

Perhaps it is unnecessary to point out that the difference between the bench and floor models is that the former stands on a workbench and the latter comes attached to its own stand (1-20 to 1-23). Purely on practical grounds, one can easily detail the advantages of bench models: they are portable, you can adjust their working height, and they can be stored away when not being used. Advantages of floor models (remember, these are generally bench models mounted on stands) are that they are stable, are permanently ready to use, and are fitted with foot switches and dust-extraction systems. Some very large machines such as those used in industrial settings would be unsuitable for bench mounting and require permanent floor stands, but since these machines are not used by the average woodworker, they will not be discussed in this book.

Standard Features of the Scroll Saw

Most scroll saws are identified by their manufacturer's name, model number, and throat capacity. Throat capacity is the distance between the blade and the frame (1-24). Other dimensions such as the stroke length and the maximum depth of cut are relevant, though frequently not even considered until some time after the machine has been

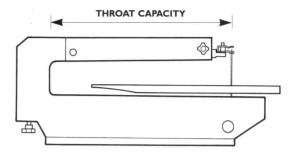

1-24. *Throat capacity is the clear distance between the back of the blade and the inside of the frame.*

acquired. The prudent prospective purchaser would do well to seek answers to questions posed in the following section Features To Consider in a Scroll Saw while inspecting the machine, in order

---

FEATURES TO CONSIDER IN A SCROLL SAW

■ **W**hat is its throat capacity, the distance between the blade and frame?

■ What is its stroke length, the distance the blade moves from the bottom to the top of its reciprocation, and is it adjustable?

■ What is the cutting speed of the scroll saw? This is specified as strokes per minute, abbreviated as spm. Does the saw have different cutting speeds, that is, is it a variable-speed saw?

■ What is its maximum depth of cut? (This is not the distance between the worktable and the underside of the upper arm at its lowest, but the maximum thickness of material recommended by the manufacturers.)

■ To what degree does the table tilt, and does it tilt to both sides or only one?

■ What is the motor power, probably stated in watts?

■ Are the blade holders suitable for plain-end and pin-end blades?

■ What extra accessories are available for this model? ■

to assess its suitability for the purpose intended.

Some of the features described in the table vary from scroll saw to scroll saw. Some of these features may not be terribly relevant to the beginner, but the more comprehensive an understanding of the scroll saw he has, the better he will be able to use it. The section that follows discusses parts that are often supplied already fitted to the machine. They vary in design and effectiveness, leaving, as always, owners to choose whichever is most appropriate to their needs. Not every machine comes with all of the listed parts as standard equipment, and, in any case, not every sawyer needs all of them. Nevertheless, when considering a particular machine, it is worth checking that these parts come with the machine. Ancillary equipment that provides additional functions and facilities appears in Chapter 2.

STROKE SPEED AND DEPTH

Stroke speed refers to the number of reciprocations by the blade counted in one minute. It is referred to as spm, an abbreviation for strokes per minute. Scroll saws at the lower end of the price range may have one speed fixed at around 1,300 to 1,500 spm, relatively high, in most opinions. Variable-speed models such as the Dremel 1695 scroll saw may operate as fast as 2,000 spm and as slow as 200 spm. Rarely do scroll saws operate at lower speeds than this, which is unfortunate, because slower speeds are desirable for more control of the cutting operation. One exception is the Diamond scroll saw, whose speed may be reduced to virtually zero.

If the class of work demands precision, remember the following rule: the more delicate the operation, the slower the speed. After all, think of the fine work possible with the hand-held fretsaw, operating at around 50 to 75 spm. It is true that, up to a point, the faster the spm the better the finish produced on the sawn sides of the work. And it is also true that if the feed rate is too slow, it is possible to burn the workpiece, due to exceptional friction, especially if the material is thick and difficult to cut. Feed rate is discussed further on page 98.

Stroke depth is the distance the frame or arms move from the top to the bottom of their stroke cycle. It is relevant because it has a bearing on the thickness of the workpiece that may be sawn. As is shown on pages 67 to 69, the design of the blade also contributes to this equation, but the primary factor is stroke depth. A scroll saw with greater stroke depth has the potential for cutting a thicker workpiece. With a stroke depth of ½ inch, for example, a scroll saw would obviously have a more difficult time cutting 1-inch-thick material than one with a 1-inch stroke. The Hegner scroll saw is noted for its adjustable stroke length, a most useful feature that allows the comfortable sawing of thin and thick materials. Several Diamond scroll saws have a 1¼-inch stroke depth, which permits the sawing of a 4-inch-thick workpiece with a suitable blade.

Illustrations 1-25 to 1-31 show how to determine and change the stroke depth on scroll saws.

SWITCHES

Most switches are positioned sensibly near the field of operation, namely the worktable (1-32). Some are beneath the table, and although they may be removed from the operator's field of vision, can be located without looking by feel with a little practice (1-33 to 1-35). Rexon produces a scroll saw that has one switch unit that switches off and turns on the saw and controls its

Text continues on page 25

1-25 (near right) and 1-26 (far right). *It is an easy matter to determine the blade-stroke depth by measuring the respective heights of the arms when raised and lowered fully. In 1-25, the arm is raised. In 1-26, the arm is lowered.*

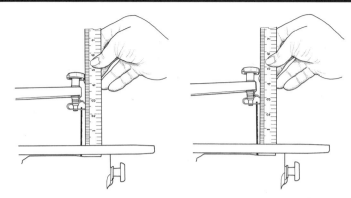

1-27 (below left). *The same method was used to ascertain the stroke depth of 1 1/4 inches on a bigger parallel-arm saw.* **1-28 (below center).** *Here the Pitman arm, with its lower bearing attached to the motor shaft, is at its lowest position. Therefore, the arm is at its closest to the table.* **1-29 (below right).** *The return stroke of the Pitman arm has raised the arm, thus increasing the distance between the arm and the table.*

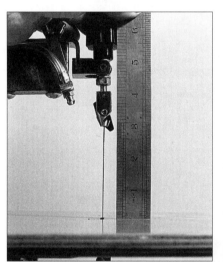  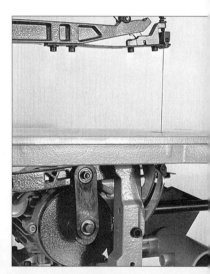

1-30 (left). *An unusual way of changing the stroke depth is available with this machine. The screw is being removed from the lower bearing to release temporarily the Pitman arm.* **1-31 (right).** *Here the Pitman arm has been moved aside to show the two positions available. Both are off-center to the spindle, to activate the reciprocation. The one furthest from the center moves the arm furthest, resulting in a larger stroke, and vice-versa. The stroke depths are from about 1/4 to 5/8 inch.*

1-32. The switch panel mounted on the outer cover of this parallel-arm machine is easy to see and operate. A convenient light is attached for local illumination of the sawing area. Variable speeds are controlled by the twist knob at the top of the switch panel.

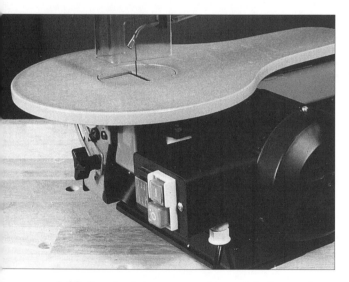

1-33. Two push buttons used to switch the scroll saw on and off are mounted beneath the worktable in a position convenient for right-hand operation.

1-34. A considerate manufacturer has included a separate power fuse that is accessed from behind the motor casing.

1-35. When the screw top is removed, the fuse is revealed for inspection.

speed and the worklight. The unit is mounted at the front of the upper arm. This is a parallel-arm scroll saw with a case that encloses the arms; thus, the switch is fixed in position.

Rocker switches are common and operate on a rocking motion from "off" to "on" for power transmission. They are usually enclosed by flexible plastic covers, presumably to keep dirt and dampness out of the circuitry (1-36). In this respect they are admirable, but they are not so easy to use because their covers make them difficult to manipulate.

A useful security measure is available on the Poolewood and Sears Craftsman scroll saws, which have a locking key which, when removed from the switch, renders the machine inoperable (1-37 and 1-38). In situations where people are learning to use scroll saws, such as in school settings, this is an important safety feature. When a scroll saw is fitted

with a variable-speed electronic control, it is an advantage if the switch controls both on/off and speed functions. Such is the case with the Dremel 1695 scroll saw. This machine also has a digital readout indicating strokes per minute.

1-37. With safety in mind, the designers have incorporated a lock in this switch.

1-38. A sensible safety device to avoid switching on the scroll saw accidentally or prevent the operating of the scroll saw by unauthorized people such as children. When the safety key is removed, it locks the switch, thus preventing its operation.

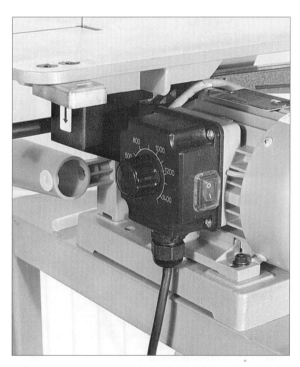

1-36. A separate rocker switch under a transparent plastic jacket starts or stops the motor. On the front of the switch box is a rotary knob for speed control.

BLADE-TENSIONING DEVICES

The blade-tensioning devices on C-frame scroll saws are less difficult to use than those on parallel-arm scroll saws because all that is required is to attach a screw-threaded blade holder to the upper frame. The screw on the holder is simply turned so that the holder is tightened against the frame, tensioning the blade in the process (1-39 to 1-42). The Poolewood scroll saw is exceptional in that it has a hinged upper part added to the otherwise normal C-frame operation. Tensioning is performed in this case by spreading the upper and lower frames apart by a screw device at the rear end.

Parallel-arm scroll saws are almost always tensioned in the saw way, that is, by drawing the rear ends of the arms together. This, in effect, spreads the front ends apart, simultaneously increasing blade tension (1-43). At least two parallel-arm scroll saws, Diamond and Hegner models have additional tensioning devices on their front ends.

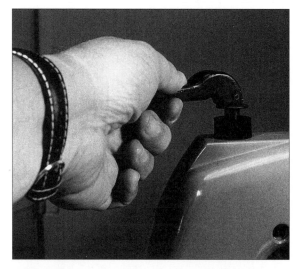

1-40. When the lever is turned, it acts as a nut, moving up or down on the threaded shaft to fine-tune the tension on the blade. When the required tension is achieved, the lever is returned to its clamping position.

1-39. Designed for blade-tensioning efficiency, this quick-acting lever is first lifted from its clamped position as shown.

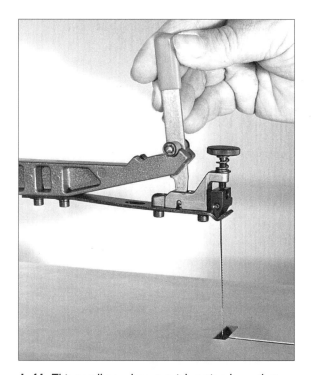

1-41. This scroll saw has a quick-acting lever that allows blade tension to be preset. With the lever in its upright position, the spring is depressed. This reduces tension on the blade, allowing it and the blade clamp to be removed or adjusted.

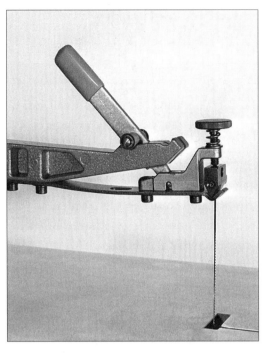

1-42. *Returning the lever to its rearward position releases downward pressure on the spring, applying preset tension to the blade.*

1-43. *Tension is applied to the blade on this parallel-arm saw by closing the distance between its rear ends.*

BLADE-TENSIONING GUIDELINES

The inexperienced scroll-saw user is often inclined to run blades at too low a tension for fear of breaking the blade. Breakage is much more likely to occur due to mishandling of materials during sawing operations than by overtensioning the blade.

Plucking the blade as a musician plucks a string is as good a way as any. When the blade is properly tensioned, it will impart certain sound or pitch, but as long as it is tight enough to give a musical note it should cut well enough. There is also the feel of resistance to the touch by the finger as the blade is plucked. If properly tensioned, it will exert a certain amount of resistance. After a few trial runs, the user will become experienced enough to judge how to adjust blade tension.

The thinner the blade, the higher the pitch for an appropriately tensioned blade. Yet, even though thinner blades have less mass, they will resist the side pressure from a finger as much as thicker blades. A useful reference for determining a blade's proper pitch is the realization that the note from a correctly tensioned blade is likely to be higher than the highest note reachable by your voice, even if you're a member of an opera club. Think of the potential gossip to be generated by neighbors when they talk of a local woodworker noted for singing to a scroll saw!

WORKTABLE TILT

A scroll saw with a worktable that can be tilted is particularly useful for bevel-sawing and inlaid work (1-44). Most machines have this feature, and allow the table to be tilted on a fulcrum coinciding with the saw-blade aperture. Generally, the table tilts down to the operator's left to at least 45 degrees when it is released from its fixed position by loosening its locking bolt. Some have a protractor scale against which a pointer may be read as the table is tilted (1-45). Securing the worktable at any desired position is easily achieved by tightening the locking bolt. Even if the model has a protractor scale, it is best to check the angle of the saw blade as   it enters the worktable by sighting-in against a geometrical protractor to ascertain its accuracy before sawing commences. (Refer to 3-70 and 3-75.) Even then, allowing for the possibility of blade flexing and misalignment of the workpiece due to operator error, it is possible to produce an incorrect angle of cut.

When setting up the worktable for normal right-angle sawing, it is best to ignore the protractor scale and set up the machine to cut square by trial and error, checking the results with the geometrical protractor. After a satisfactory result is attained, examine the pointer to

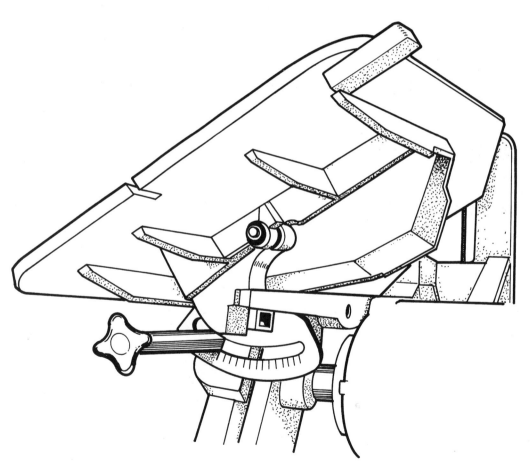

I-44. *The table on this scroll saw is tilted for bevel- or miter-cutting. The star knob is used to clamp the table at the desired angle.*

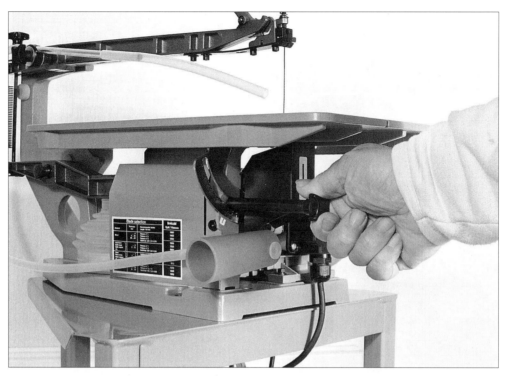

1-45. *An extended shaft on the adjuster knob makes for greater ease when operating the table lock. A protractor is incorporated in the table-tilting assembly.*

see if it registers with the "zero" mark on the scale. If not, the pointer may be adjusted accordingly. Mercifully, when scales are fitted, manufacturers usually include an adjustable pointer. Some even go to the trouble of furnishing the system of adjustment with a register on which the table will rest when it is returned to its normal working position, obviating the need to check it every time it is returned from a tilted angle.

DUST BLOWER

Because the dust blower's effectiveness is debatable, it does not always come fitted as standard equipment on scroll saws. Most machines have simple cylindrical bellows positioned in direct contact with the frame (1-46 and 1-47). As the frame reciprocates the bellows are activated,

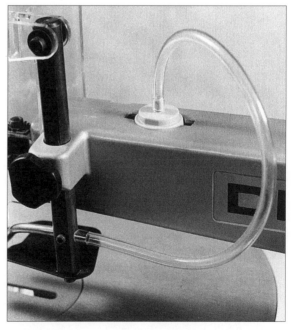

1-46. *The bellows outlet is connected by plastic tube to the nozzle housed in the hold-down shaft.*

1-47. The blower-nozzle is fixed in position by a grub screw housed in the hold-down shaft.

creating a puff of air that clears the dust from the sawing area. The bellows, of course, also draw in air, but do not have sufficient power to suck away the dust.

Often, the dust blower's orifice is oriented such that it blows the dust toward the operator. Its main function is to clear the saw path, leaving the line or mark visible to the operator. It is, of course, possible to keep the area clear by exhaling strongly and blowing away the dust as it is created. This, however, is somewhat tiresome. Angling the blower orifice to blow the dust away from the operator may be possible, and that is probably the best compromise.

If the scroll saw is fitted with a dust chute,

connect it to a vacuum cleaner or dust extractor. This will clear debris that falls from the table or is drawn down by the blade. At least one scroll saw—a Hegner model—has a device that reconnects the blower tube from the bellows to a vacuum tube to draw dust from the immediate sawing area. This is to comply with certain safety regulations.

HOLD-DOWN

As its name indicates, the function of a hold-down is to prevent the workpiece from being lifted off the table by the saw blade on the upstroke of the frame (1-48 and 1-49). It is an essential piece of equipment for a beginner, who may have trouble manipulating the workpiece while simultaneously holding it down.

Ideally, the hold-down can be adjusted not merely up and down to suit various thicknesses of material (1-50), but also at angles to the table if bevels are being sawn (1-51). Many hold-downs have a built-in guard to help prevent accidental contact of the fingers with the moving blade (1-52). Many experienced sawyers shun the use of either, not because they are foolhardy or careless, but because they have better access to the workpiece and are better able to manipulate it without the hold-down and guard. Also, it is fair to say that the scroll saw is, relative to other power tools, not dangerous, and the user may quickly learn to work with as few accessories as possible. However, if using a hold-down ensures a feeling of security, use it. If just learning how to operate a scroll saw, also use a hold-down. See Hold-Down on pages 42 to 45 for more information on optional hold-downs.

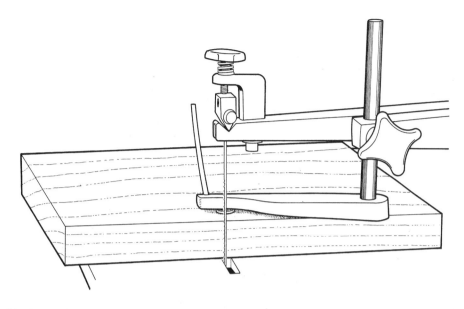

1-48. This hold-down is resting in place on the workpiece to prevent it from rising during sawing. Note the upright rod that acts as a guard to protect fingers from the blade.

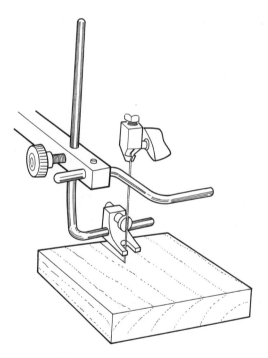

1-49. A forked hold-down that has a blade support. The blade support is in contact with the back of the blade to prevent it from being deformed during sawing, especially when hardwoods or metals are being cut. The Z bar mounted to the front of the blade guards the fingers.

1-50. The height of this hold-down is adjusted by moving the shaft to which it is attached. When the desired position is reached, the carrier shaft is locked by tightening the knob on the end of the fixed arm.

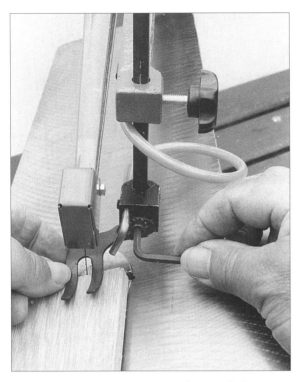

I-51. This forked hold-down can be swiveled to suit the tilt of the table for bevel-sawing.

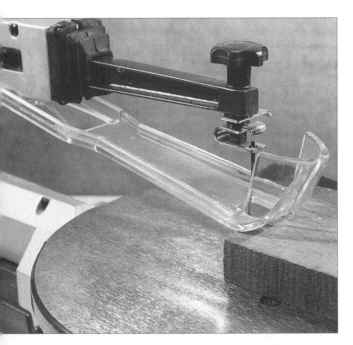

I-52. A simple but effective hold-down, which doubles as a guard, maintains downward pressure on the workpiece by a constant built-in spring action.

GUARDS

When guards are fitted as separate items from the hold-down, they are usually made from transparent plastic (1-53 to 1-55). This allows uninterrupted sight of the sawing action and also adds a barrier between the blade and the eyes. Hazards of this kind are dealt with in Chapter 8.

If the guard is fitted on a swing hinge—and it usually is—general wear and tear will cause scratches on it that makes its surface difficult to see through. In this case, it may be helpful to add a little knob on the side for handling (1-56). This reduces contact with the plastic on the guard, therefore preserving for as long as possible the guard's transparency.

Refer to Chapter 8 for more information on using guards.

I-53. Transparent plastic guards allow the sawing operation to be viewed while helping to prevent accidental contact with the blade.

1-54. *When changing blades or working with a small workpiece, the guard can be lifted for access without being detached from the scroll saw.*

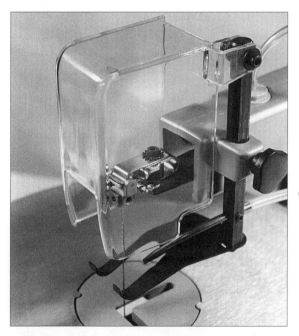

1-55. *A variation on the see-through guard is this molded-plastic version. It also hinges vertically for greater access.*

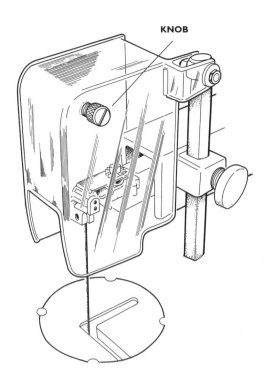

1-56. *To avoid damage to the surface of a transparent plastic hold-down, a small knob may be attached for handling. A hole 1/32 of an inch less than the diameter of the screw thread should be drilled in the plastic before the knob is screwed in, to avoid splitting the material.*

STORAGE BOX

A storage box that stores blades, keys, and other small items comes as standard equipment with some scroll saws (1-57). This may be attached to the machine in some convenient location, and fitted with a hinged lid.

BLADE-BREAKAGE DEVICE

It is worth knowing if a scroll saw is fitted with a device that stops the reciprocating movement of the arms if the blade breaks (1-58). This is a thoughtful feature that prevents the operator's fingers from being cut by the broken blade end.

1-57. A useful storage box is attached to the rear casing of this saw. It allows storage for spare blades and other small accessories.

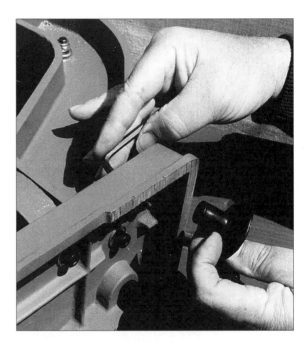

1-59. Rubber feet help to stabilize scroll saws and reduce vibration and noise. Rubber feet are fine for a temporary location but the saw is better operated if bolted to the work surface.

RUBBER FEET

A few considerate manufacturers include rubber feet to add to the scroll saw for occasions when it will not be bolted down to a workbench (1-59). The Poolewood scroll saw, for instance, being a relatively heavy machine, performs securely on its rubber feet without needing to be bolted down if it is being used in one location temporarily. A bonus is the reduction in vibration and sound. Rubber feet are also included with the Diamond scroll saw.

TABLE INSERTS

Replaceable table inserts are a good idea in cases where inserts wear out excessively, but only if the inserts are of the correct thickness to ensure that the table surface is level (1-60 and 1-61). Any irregularity of the work surface caused because

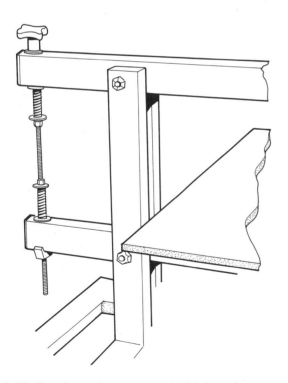

1-58. This device for tensioning the blade incorporates the safety feature that stops and raises the upper arm if the blade breaks.

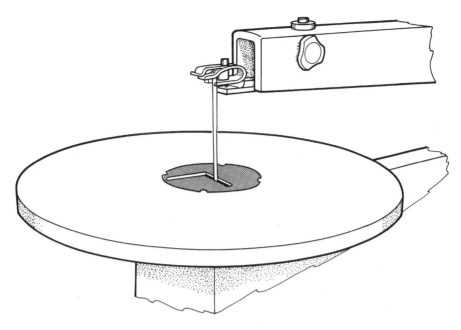

1-60. *A replaceable circular table insert that can be removed and repositioned to suit the blade location. With this type of blade holder, the blade can be used to cut forwards or sideways.*

1-61. *Design features of the table insert include slotted holes to allow blade clearance while the table is inclined.*

the table and the insert are of different thickness is undesirable. If the insert is too thin, more material should be added to it. If it is too thick, it should be reduced. Many perils await the sawyer who attempts to produce good work from an imperfect table surface.

Maintaining Scroll-Saw Components

Scroll saws are simple machines that require little in the way of servicing. Therefore, there is little excuse for ignoring the few maintenance procedures, which are listed below:

1. Clean and lubricate the moving parts regularly. Bearings in pivot points need more lubrication than others (1-62 to 1-65). All parts that rub against others are subject to potential wear no matter how well-made they may be. Some careful inspection should reveal these parts.

Text continues on page 38

MAINTENANCE TECHNIQUES

1-62. Regular lubrication is an essential part of the maintenance schedule. Motor spindle bearings are hard-worked parts.

1-63. Pivots have to be lubricated lightly and frequently. The manufacturer of these bearings claim that they are "sealed for life." Whose life?

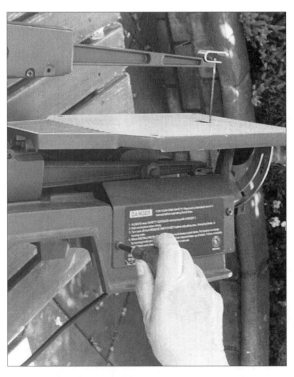

1-64 and 1-65 (following page). Maintaining the parts on a Sears parallel-arm scroll saw. Here the inspection cover retained by two screws is being removed to get to the parts.

MAINTENANCE TECHNIQUES (CONTINUED)

1-65. *The bearings on the Pitman arm connecting the drive to the arm need regular attention with a light machine oil in order to reduce wear on these much-worked components.*

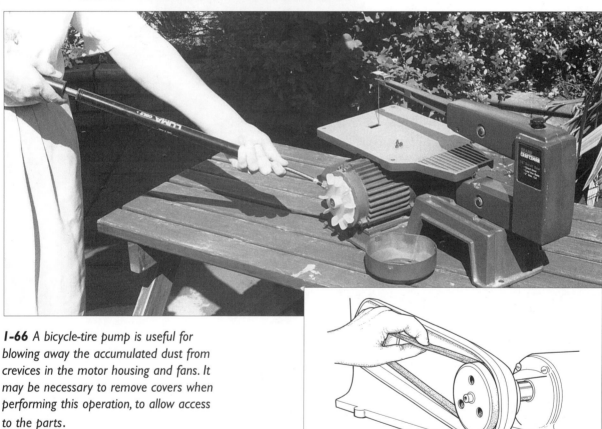

1-66 *A bicycle-tire pump is useful for blowing away the accumulated dust from crevices in the motor housing and fans. It may be necessary to remove covers when performing this operation, to allow access to the parts.*

1-67. *Drive belts should be checked to ensure that they are secure, correctly seated on the pulleys, and of sufficient tension to drive without slipping. Inspection for wear should also be carried out at this time.*

2. Clean air vents in the motor casings regularly, because they are vulnerable to blockage by dust deposits. A cycle pump or air line is good for this. If these items are not available, use a soft artist's brush or a strip of material wrapped around a small stick (1-66).

3. If the scroll saw has a dust blower, make sure the air inlet is clear and drawing air in freely.

4. Occasionally wipe the parts of the scroll saw that are made of bare metal (such as a cast steel table) with something that fights corrosion and inhibits rust, to ensure long-term protection of these parts. These components are very vulnerable to rust, even in favorable atmospheric conditions.

5. Check drive belts, connecting rods, and any other linkages, looking for signs of wear. Replace the parts that are defective immediately, if possible, to prevent accumulative damage to other parts (1-67).

6. Remove, oil, and replace all screws and nuts from time to time. This necessitates a complete inspection, making you familiar with how the machine works and its current condition. There are countless scroll saws in use that are more than a quarter of a century old. This is testimony to the importance of regular maintenance.

2 Accessories

As was mentioned in the earlier section entitled Standard Features of the Scroll Saw on pages 21-35, there are many other accessories that are available as "optional extras." Very often, these accessories are much more effective than the standard components and within a short time of acquiring them seem to become essential.

Some of these accessories can be easily made by the scroll-sawyer. In some cases, these user-made accessories are better than those available from the manufacturers. Others are unobtainable from manufacturers, and, therefore, have to be user made. Each of these accessories is described below.

The following accessories are broken down into two groups: miscellaneous optional accessories and jigs.

Miscellaneous Optional Accessories

FOOT SWITCH

There is an element of controversy about the subject of foot switches (2-1). Some woodworkers are opposed to their use, while others are in favor. There are merits to both arguments. Some points made against the use of foot switches are that: 1, the switch can be unintentionally activated if the operator accidentally steps on it; and 2, there is the potential that the operator

2-1. The foot switch, which frees the operator's hands to operate the workpiece, is connected between the power supply and the machine motor. Accidental activation of the foot switch can be avoided by raising it off the floor. It would be prudent to raise the one shown here even more by attaching it to a wooden platform.

will be using an insecure stance because the leg operating the switch will not be properly braced.

Operators in favor of the foot switch refute these considerations by arguing that: 1, the risk of unintentionally activating the foot switch can be avoided by raising it above the level of the floor, either on a raised block or attached somewhere on the machine stand; and 2, the operator's cutting stance can be secured by sitting down. Additional points in favor of using a foot switch are that both hands are left free to manipulate the workpiece without the distraction of operating the switch, and that the scroll saw's speed can be adjusted, during the sawing operation, if a variable-speed control is incorporated into the foot switch.

In this writer's opinion, the advantages far outweigh the disadvantages. Many sawing operations, such as bevel-sawing with a tilted worktable, delicate hole-cutting, etc., are made more efficient and secure with a foot switch.

DUST-EXTRACTION UNIT

A dust-extractor unit does *not* mean a vacuum extraction port attached to the scroll saw in the hope of drawing debris from the sawing area, but a unit purposely designed for the scroll saw. Hegner has produced such a unit in answer to recent safety requirements regarding the control of sawdust. It is an accessory that is even more efficient than the bellows blower (2-2 to 2-4). The tube on this unit that delivers the air can be operated in reverse so that it withdraws the dust. In short, the tube "sucks in" rather than "blows away" the dust. Bolted onto the machine is a molded unit incorporating an extraction port intended to accept a tube connected to a vacuum cleaner or similar device. The tube, described above, is disconnected from the bellows and inserted into the vacuum unit. Since there is an inlet hole in the vacuum unit positioned beneath the hole in the worktable, the tube collects falling sawdust and draws it into the vacuum. The inlet end of the tube, positioned close to the saw

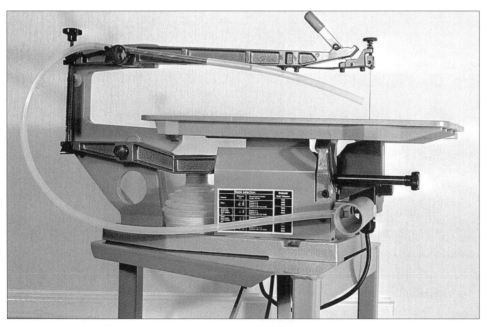

2-2. An unusual accessory is fitted to the extractor port underneath the table. A plastic tube that normally fits into the bellows housing at the rear acts as an extractor tube to draw sawdust away from the sawing area.

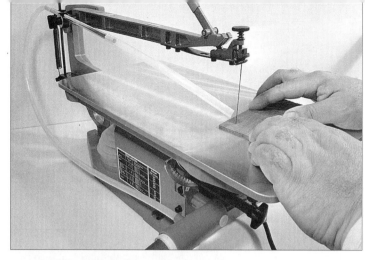

2-3. As sawdust falls through the table, it is drawn into the open end of the extractor port and into the vacuum tube. Dust accumulating on the top of the workpiece is drawn into the plastic tube, whose open end is placed very close to the saw-blade entry point.

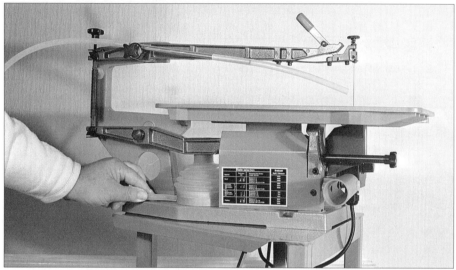

2-4. If it is necessary to discontinue use of the dust-extractor unit, disconnect the plastic tube from the extractor port and insert it into the bellows outlet. This returns the system to the standard blower function.

blade, now sucks in rather than blows away the dust, and should be attached to the vacuum so that it is close enough to draw away dust as it is produced by the sawing operation.

FLEXIBLE SHAFT

The flexible shaft or drive, which is used to drive drill bits and other accessories such as spindle-mounted buffers, abrasives, or cutters, is available for very few scroll saws. One scroll saw with this facility is the Diamond scroll saw, which features a connection close to the on-off switch. The connection accepts the drive shaft of the power take-off. A grub screw is used to lock the drive shaft in position (2-5 and 2-6). At the ter-

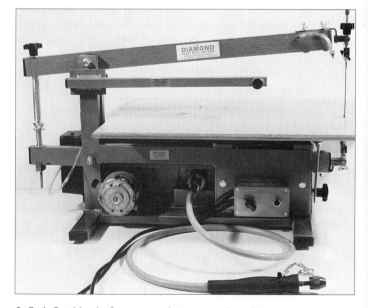

2-5. A flexible shaft connected at one end to the power take-off on the scroll saw.

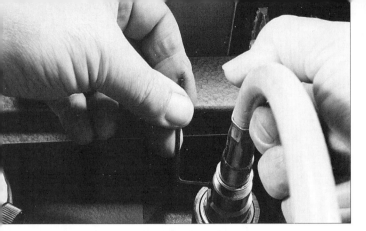

2-6. *The flexible shaft spindle is inserted into the power take-off. A grub screw is tightened on the spindle with a socket key.*

2-8. *A drill is used to bore access holes for the insertion of blades when cutting internal work or holes in workpieces.*

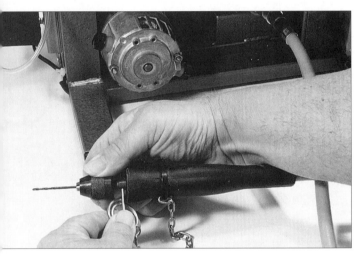

2-7. *The flexible drive is fitted with a conventional three-jaw chuck. It is operated with the left hand to lock the drive spindle, and the right hand to tighten the collar.*

2-9. *Many bits, cutters, or abrading tools can be fitted into the chuck on the flexible shaft. In this example, a small abrasive drum is held in the chuck to chamfer a sharp corner.*

minal of the drive is a three-jaw drill chuck intended for manual operation (2-7). The flexible drive is a convenient tool for drilling access holes for blades, cutting apertures, or, if necessary, smoothing ragged edges on workpieces (2-8 and 2-9).

HOLD-DOWNS

Not all machines come with hold-downs as standard equipment. This is because not all sawyers use them. It is not unusual to find that the hold-down design may (some may say, sensibly) include a safety guard to help protect the fingers from blade contact. This is the case with the Hegner hold-down. The arm carrying the hold-down is attached to the upper, parallel arm of the scroll saw, and is adjusted laterally, while the height of the foot is adjusted by raising or lowering it on its vertical shaft (2-10 to 2-12). The hold-down contacts the workpiece on one

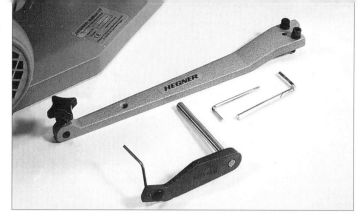

2-10. The hold-down disassembled, showing its arm and foot.

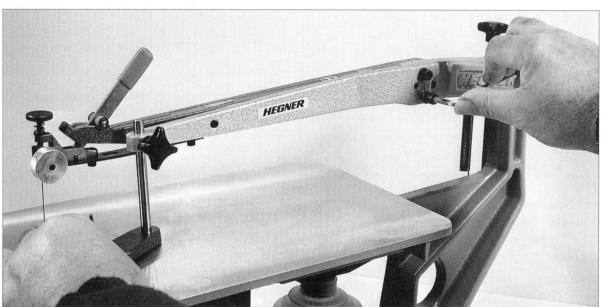

2-11. Anchoring the hold-down to the rigid rear pillar of the scroll saw ensures that the arm and hold-down remain immobile.

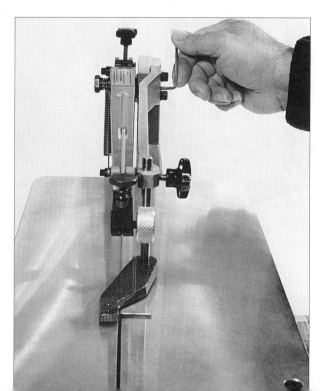

2-12 (left). Adjustment of the grub screw applies leverage that changes the angle of orientation of the hold-down arm.

of its sides. A plain, upright rod rises out of the foot and is positioned in front of the blade to prevent fingers from touching the blade (2-13).

Diamond's hold-down has a fork-shaped foot that spans the blade and allows contact with the workpiece around the blade (2-14 and 2-15). There are many ways to adjust the hold-down. A sensible feature is the incorporation of a pressure pad intended to be brought against the back of the blade as a support to prevent it from deflection (2-16 and 2-17).

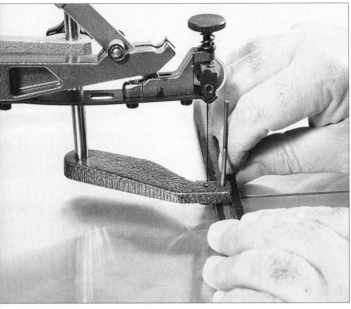

2-14. The components of this hold-down include a guard and pressure pad for the blade.

2-13. The hold-down has two functions. It prevents the workpiece from rising on the up-stroke of the blade, and its foot has an upright rod that helps to prevent accidental contact of the fingers with the blade.

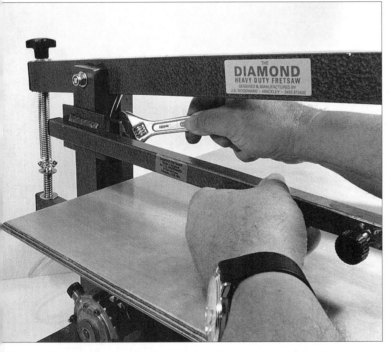

2-15. Support of the hold-down arm is provided by the rear pillar of the scroll saw to which the hold-down is bolted.

2-16. Incorporated in the foot of the hold-down is a pressure pad, adjustable fore-and-aft to allow contact with the blade.

2-17. *During the sawing operation, deflection of the blade is prevented by the pressure pad. At the end of the arm is the adjustable guard which prevents the fingers from coming into contact with the blade. Its guard rail runs horizontally and effectively in front of the blade.*

2-18. *Smoothing rough surfaces may not be the first priority of the scroll saw, but it may be a very useful supplementary function, particularly if a large amount of light sanding is needed. An emery board, confiscated from a fingernail cosmetic kit, makes an admirable abrasive. The swivel feature of the blade holder depicted allows frontal pressure and also allows the emory board to be rotated 180 degrees, so that the alternate, coarser face of the emery board may be used.*

ACCESSORIES FOR ABRADING WOOD

Several accessories are available that can convert the scroll saw from a machine that cuts wood to one that smooths wood. It should be realized that the scroll saw can in no way replace a disc or belt sander, but rather should be used as a means of gently smoothing delicate surfaces in situations where two hands on the workpiece are better than one. Where it is normal, for example, to hold the piece in one hand while smoothing it with the other, the scroll saw may be the answer.

Some varieties of files lend themselves admirably to this task, including those coated in so-called "diamonds" or "sapphires." Less expensive and, in some ways, better for the workshop are the type made from materials similar to woodworking abrasives, referred to usually as "emery boards" (2-18). They frequently come with coarse and fine grits, permitting a choice of different abrasive qualities on one board without the need to change it for another. Since there is

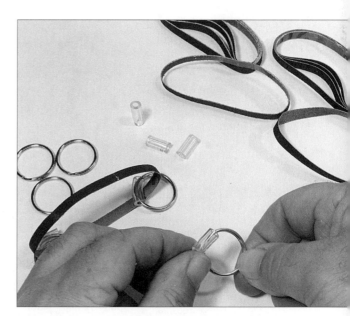

2-19. *Flexible bands coated with abrasive grit are attached to split rings that are cushioned with plastic sleeves.*

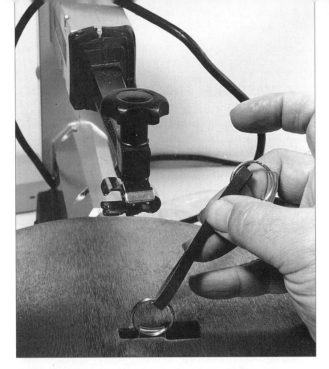

2-20. *Held in the clamps designed for stirrup-type blade holders, the bands can be tightened like blades, but to a lower tension, of course.*

2-22. *High-speed action with a light touch achieves a very smooth finish, producing a polished surface if needed.*

2-21. *Plastic sleeves cushion the bands against the split rings to reduce stress. This arrangement allows rotation of the bands to expose unused areas to extend their usability.*

2-23. *If a particular scroll saw is not equipped with the stirrup-type blade holders, it is possible to add an improvised, shop-made extension hook to the band-fitting kit. This extension hook was made from a piece of wire coat hanger and bent with pliers. Size and shape of hooks will depend on the type of blade holder with which the machine is equipped.*

no directional arrangement of the abrasive, unlike the teeth on a scroll-saw blade, the emery board may be reversed to utilize both ends.

A recent development is the abrasive loops made from coated cloth that are attached to split rings. The split rings are attached to the blade holder (2-19). A useful characteristic of these abrasive loops is their flexibility; the lower the tension applied by the scroll-saw arms, the more flexible the loop (2-20 and 2-21). A range of grits is available, and these are as applicable to metals and other materials as to wood. Using fine grades allows a surface to be polished, if required (2-22 and 2-23).

MACHINE STAND

As was mentioned earlier, a bench-top scroll saw can be converted to a floor model when it is attached to a stand. (See 1-20 to 1-23 on page 20.) The advantages and disadvantages depend on many aspects of the individual environment that affect the scroll saw and its user. If the machine is going to be used frequently and permanent space is available, then there is a good case for mounting the scroll saw on a stand. This means that the machine is then fixed at whatever height is dictated by the stand, thus bringing up the question if it is better to operate the machine while standing or sitting. While the operator can sit on a high stool to operate a free-standing scroll saw, a low stand designed for sitting if used standing would probably require an uncomfortable stooping stance. The question posed, therefore, is how much time will be spent at any one sawing session? What may be regarded as a long period of time by one person may not be to another, but certainly any length of time spent on the feet is tiring if the body is relatively immobile. Another consideration in favor of sitting, aside from comfort, is that the sawyer is better able to use a foot switch to start or stop the scroll saw.

Refer to Bench or Floor Models? on page 21 for more on machine stands.

MAGNIFIER

Delicate work demands close-up scrutiny and, regardless of the operators age and eyesight, some magnification is an advantage. Since the operator's hand will be occupied in the careful manipulation of the workpiece, it follows that a hands-free magnifier is obligatory. A magnifier that also has a light is doubly beneficial (2-24 to 2-26).

2-24. *Magnification is an advantage to the sawyer making delicate or precise cuts or making miniatures. It is even better if the magnifier also has a light.*

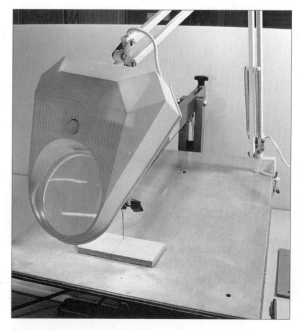

2-25. *Illumination improves visibility at the sawing area without dazzling, because the light unit is shielded from the user.*

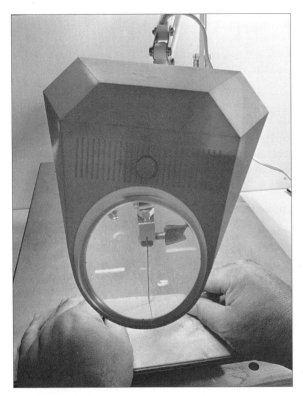

2-26. A view through the lens shows a well-lit and magnified work area.

Freestanding magnifiers have substantial bases to ensure their stability. These bases have to support a hinged arrangement that allows for universal adjustment of the magnifier/light unit. Unfortunately, the base is too large to be accommodated on the worktable, so it should be placed within easy reach on an adjacent bench or surface near to the scroll saw.

Other types of magnifiers have detachable brackets that are used to attach the unit temporarily to a stable platform. Again, due to the need to keep the table uncluttered, it is best to find a location close to, but not on, the worktable.

VIBRATION ABSORPTION MAT

Designed to be used for any bench-top power tool, these mats absorb vibration and reduce noise by isolating the machine from the hard work surface (2-27 and 2-28). Another advantage is that they grip the bench top and prevent the tool from moving. These mats are particularly useful when the scroll saw is used temporarily in a specific work location.

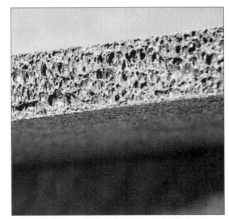

2-28. The cellular structure of the mat produces resistance to vibration and reduces sound transmission.

2-27. Whether or not it is bolted down, the vibration absorption mat helps keep the scroll saw stable and reduces noise that would otherwise be transmitted to the workbench. In a temporary workplace, provided no hefty work is planned, the mat helps to prevent the machine from sliding.

2-29. *The Tool-Bridge is a complete accessory for the serious sawing of very demanding and precise work, especially miniature pieces and light metal. It consists of several components. Shown here is the base unit and bridge clamped to the table.*

ACCESSORY FOR CUTTING THIN WOOD OR METAL

The Tool-Bridge is an accessory developed by Diamond that is used for precision work involving thin wood or metals. It is fixed to the table by clamps (spring clamps are adequate). The Tool-Bridge consists of the bridge itself, a pair of hold-downs, a pressure pad that is fitted on its back, an ancillary dust-blower nozzle, and magnifying lens, all independently adjustable for maximum coordination (2-29 to 2-33). Whether it is used for the production of metal parts or for fine woodwork, both cases where accuracy is essential, the Tool-Bridge is unbeatable. Refer to Cutting metal on pages 107 and 108 for more information.

2-30. *The pressure pad on the shaft fitted on the bridge has been brought into contact with the blade to prevent its rearward deflection under pressure. It is adjusted so that the blade runs clear when not cutting. Fast-change holders are fitted as a complement to the assembly.*

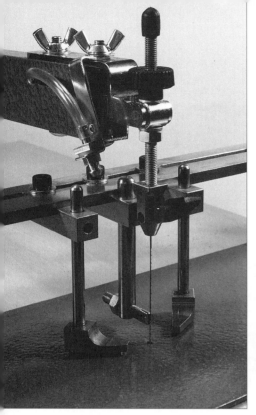

2-31. *On either side of the pressure pad are two separate feet independently adjustable for height and width.*

2-32. *A plastic tube fits through the hold-down arm, unused in conjunction with this arrangement, and is connected to the air pump and the nozzle to bring air close to the work area. This air blows away any debris.*

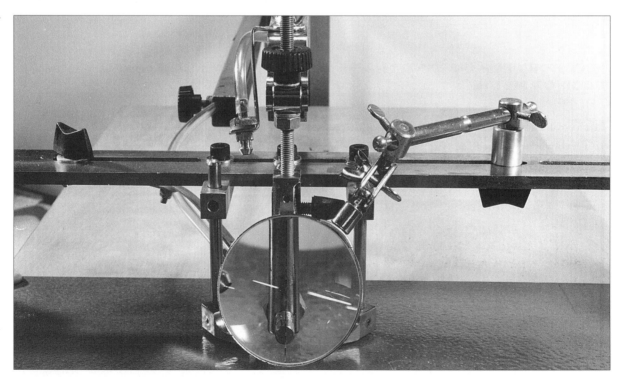

2-33. *Universal adjustment of the magnifying lens makes close work a pleasure.*

2-34. *A coolant dispenser is an important accessory for any sawyer cutting quantities of metal. Under the bench is a reservoir connected to a foot pump that sends measured pulses of coolant to the cutting area.*

COOLANT DISPENSER

One indispensable aid when cutting metal is a means by which coolant can be supplied to the blade during the sawing process (2-34 and 2-35). If this is of the type supplied by Hegner, it has a remote-control foot pump that allows the coolant to be supplied precisely to the blade without interrupting the sawing operation.

Refer to Cutting Metal on pages 107 and 108 for more information.

BLADE CONTAINER

There are transparent tubular containers available that have been specifically made for the safe storage of blades and other small parts. These containers have tight-fitting lids intended to exclude harmful dust and dampness. The lids have small loops for hanging if desired, and the transparent material means that it is not necessary to empty out the contents for visual inspection (2-36).

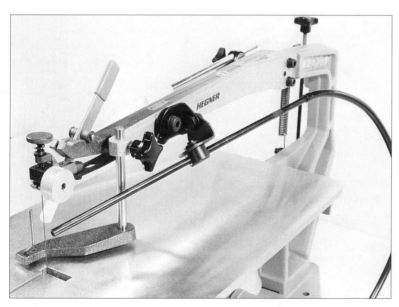

2-35. *The rubber tube is connected to the metal terminal fitted to the hold-down arm. Precise location of the coolant terminal is available by using the universal bracket.*

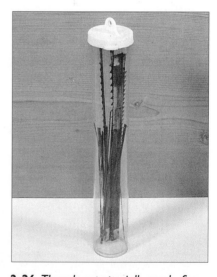

2-36. *Though not specially made for scroll-saw-blade storage, this container is perfectly suitable because it is of the proper size and transparent. It may be hung up by the loop on the top of the lid.*

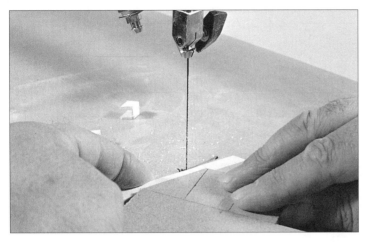

2-37. *Cutting pieces of channel for blade storage. The white plastic channel is held by the left hand across the end of the sliding block, which is controlled by the right hand.*

2-40. *As many channel dividers as necessary can be glued to the blade rack.*

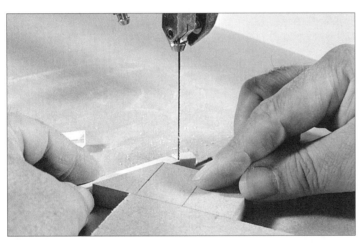

2-38. *As the right hand pushes the sliding block forward, the left hand supports the channel as it is sawn. A fixed block is clamped on the worktable at the preset angle to provide guidance for the sliding block.*

2-39 (below). *Trimmed to length and at the correct angle, the piece of channel may now be joined to the other channels.*

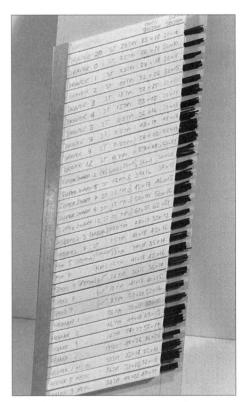

2-41. *Each piece of channel when glued to adjacent ones provides a pocket about ¹/4 inch square, sufficient capacity for a dozen or more blades.*

Plastic tubing produced for domestic services may be acquired to achieve the same result as the store-bought type. This may be cut to the required length and end-stops may be used as lids (2-37 to 2-41).

The blade rack shown in 2-40 provides a means to separate and quickly identify blades. This storage container is normally kept in a drawer under the workbench with a bag or two of silica to keep corrosion at bay. A magnetic pad is a useful way to store blades (2-42). It holds blades neatly near the machine.

Magnetic pads are available in a variety of sizes. One about 2 x 6 inches wide makes a very practical means of keeping blades and other small objects handy. The pad can be fixed by adhesive to a wall, bench top, or other surface convenient to the user.

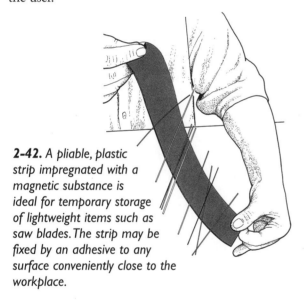

2-42. *A pliable, plastic strip impregnated with a magnetic substance is ideal for temporary storage of lightweight items such as saw blades. The strip may be fixed by an adhesive to any surface conveniently close to the workplace.*

GEOMETRICAL PROTRACTOR

Not all machines come with a built-in protractor that can be used to check table settings, bevels, and miters, so a hand-held type may be necessary (2-43).

There is a wide selection of protractors from which to choose that may be confusing, but some are produced especially for the scroll-saw

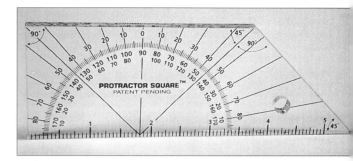

2-43. *A geometrical protractor, made from material thick enough to allow it to stand freely on the worktable. Because it is transparent, both its divisions and the saw blade can be seen simultaneously. Peripheral angles include 45, 90, and 135 degrees.*

user. A protractor that can be used freestanding, leaving the hands free to make adjustments, is beneficial when leveling the worktable to square-up the blade angle.

AWLS FOR HOLE-BORING

Access holes for saw blades have to be drilled into workpieces if any internal cutting is needed. If the hole is likely to be visible after the saw has passed (and this may depend somewhat on the size of the blade), then the smaller the hole the better. Establishing the minimum-size hole is a matter of trial and error with some scrap material.

A user-made bodkin, or awl, provides a simple means of boring holes (2-44). If it is tapered, it

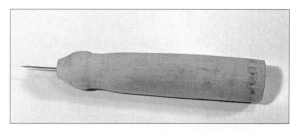

2-44. *A user-made awl, or bodkin, used to pierce thin workpieces. It is ideal for boring holes in veneers or other thin work where very fine blades are used. The steel point, a sewing needle, was glued into a simple wooden handle with epoxy resin.*

will allow some graduation in the achievable sizes of holes. A bodkin can consist of a typical sewing needle inserted into a wooden handle. It is best to glue, with epoxy adhesive, the needle into a prepared hole in the handle, thus preventing it from detaching or gradually penetrating into the handle.

Miniature Archimedes drills are ideal for drilling access holes (2-45). Their small chucks accept small-diameter bits and even sharpened panel pins and brads that, if suitably filed or ground, make perfectly acceptable drill bits.

2-45. An Archimedean drill with a spiral shaft that rotates when the spool is traversed back and forth. In the chuck is a user-made bit made from a brad.

A sensible step to cut down on test-drilling holes is to measure the width of the blade to assess the diameter of a suitable drill (2-46). It is not difficult to obtain sets of small-diameter drill bits from model-making suppliers. Some come in containers that double conveniently as storage receptacles and drill holders (2-47 and 2-48). In practice, it is possible to fit a blade into a hole of slightly less diameter than its thickness. If a blade measures .022 or .025 inch, try it in a hole .020 inch in diameter, and it will probably enter with a little persuasion (2-49 to 2-51).

DETERMINING AND MAKING BLADE-ENTRY HOLES

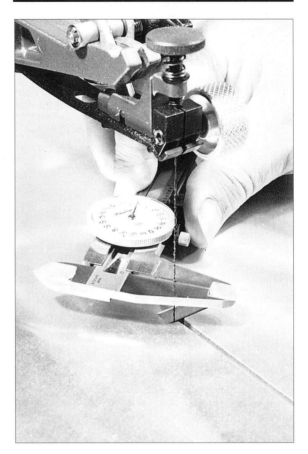

2-46. Checking the maximum width of a blade to establish the diameter of the least conspicuous access hole.

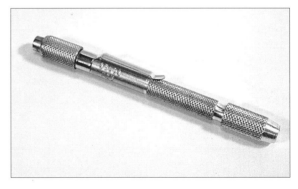

2-47. A compact drill set housed in a dual-purpose holder.

DETERMINING AND MAKING
BLADE-ENTRY HOLES (CONTINUED)

2-48. *Ten bits are stored in the four-piece holder that consists of a hollow shaft, a collet, a chuck sleeve, and a magnetic cap.*

2-49. *A knurled surface finish on the shaft of the drill holder gives a good grip for rotation of the bit.*

2-50. *At around .020 inch in diameter, the drill bit bores through the 1/8-inch wood panel swiftly and cleanly.*

2-51. *The .022-inch blade enters easily with only slight binding at its corners. There is little gap between the blade and the hole.*

Jigs

STRAIGHT FENCE

A fence is the kind of accessory that is most frequently associated with circular saws, band saws, etc., but it is perfectly feasible to use a fence with the scroll saw if a quantity of parallel strips is required (2-52 to 2-54). The fence, once set up correctly, permits parallel items to be sawn without the need to measure and mark them off with a straightedge. Whether made for a special task or improvised from a length of wood clamped

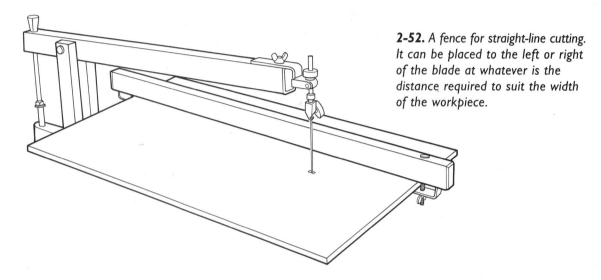

2-52. A fence for straight-line cutting. It can be placed to the left or right of the blade at whatever is the distance required to suit the width of the workpiece.

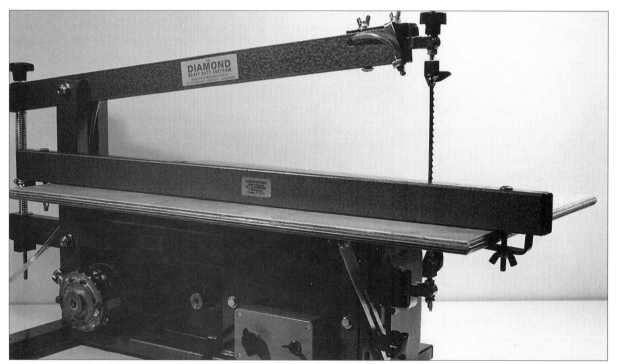

2-53. Not a common accessory, the straight fence fitted to this machine permits repetitive cutting of parallel strips.

2-54. *The fence is attached to the scroll saw by using the wing nuts on a bracket to clamp it to the table.*

to the worktable, a straight fence is a helpful accessory.

Regardless of the type of fence used, it is essential to understand a fundamental characteristic of all scroll-saw blades: their tendency to cut towards one side. If the workpiece were to be pushed in a straight line at the blade, it would veer off and not follow a line parallel to the line of movement. Disaster would ensue, resulting in a loss of contact with the marked line or a broken blade. It is recommended to take this tendency into account rather than trying to force the unwilling blade into submission.

Establishing the angle of deviation is easy if this simple method is followed. Take a piece of scrap wood with a straight side and mark a line parallel to its edge. Saw along the line for a short distance, say an inch, steering the workpiece to ensure that the blade follows the line accurately. To achieve this, the workpiece will undoubtedly have to be angled out toward the operator's right hand, this being the blade's normal bias. Stop the operation at this point,

and hold the workpiece at this angle. Next, use a pencil to mark a line on the table along the edge of the workpiece. Then put the workpiece aside and set a sliding bevel at the angle indicated by the pencil line. If the fence is arranged at this angle, it should be a straightforward process to cut parallel pieces at whatever width the fence is fixed.

An alternative way to establish the angle of deviation is to set up the fence at the required width from the blade and estimate the angle, or even to set the fence parallel with the table edge if the edge is straight. Saw a test piece using the fence at that setting and note the width achieved at each end (2-55). The difference, assuming that there is one, should indicate not only the width differential but also the deviation in angle. Adjust the fence to compensate for the deviation in angle and begin sawing (2-56 to 2-58).

It is worth mentioning that a consistent pressure on the workpiece is essential if the angular bias is to be maintained. If the forward pressure on the blade varies, the deviation and parallelism could be lost.

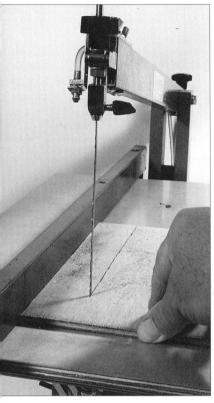

2-55. A trial cut is made using the fence at the desired width.

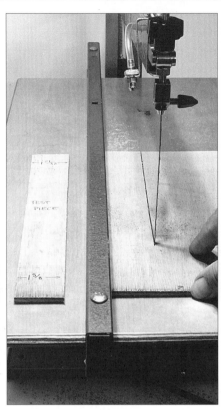

2-56. Having measured the test piece at each end to verify that they are parallel to each other, the operator next adjusts the fence to correct any misalignment.

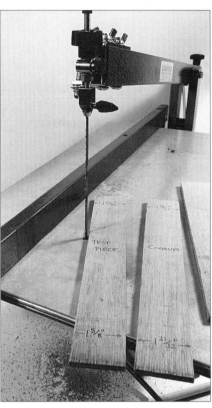

2-57. Sawing is now possible at this fence setting.

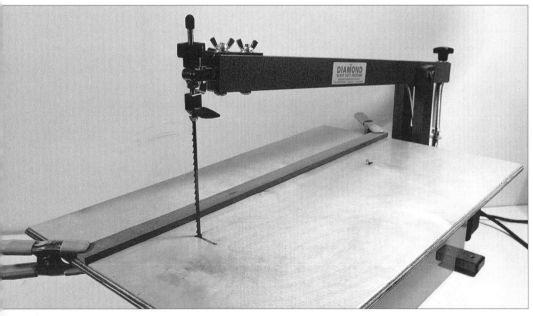

2-58. An arrangement similar to the purposely built fence can be improvised with a straight strip of wood, provided that it is wider than it is deep, to prevent lateral deflection of the blade.

FINGER FENCE

A finger fence is an accessory that has been "borrowed" from band-saw operators. Band-saw blades also have a tendency to cut towards one side, and often cause trouble if hefty sections are being handled against a guiding fence. The finger fence is used to correct this deviation either for straight-line sawing or for curved profile work (2-59).

Usually made from waste wood of appropriate proportions, finger fences are invariably made to specific dimensions by the user and clamped temporarily to the worktable. Even if used infre-

quently, they are worth having and take little time to make. They are at their best when used for cutting parallel curves (2-60 to 2-63). It is important to set them level with the point at which the blade enters the material, on a line square to the line of travel of the workpiece. The first cut to establish the required curve must be made freehand, of course. Having sawn the desired profile, the operator simply steers the workpiece into the blade using the finger fence. A little practice is recommended prior to embarking on a lengthy production run, with occasional inspection to check accuracy.

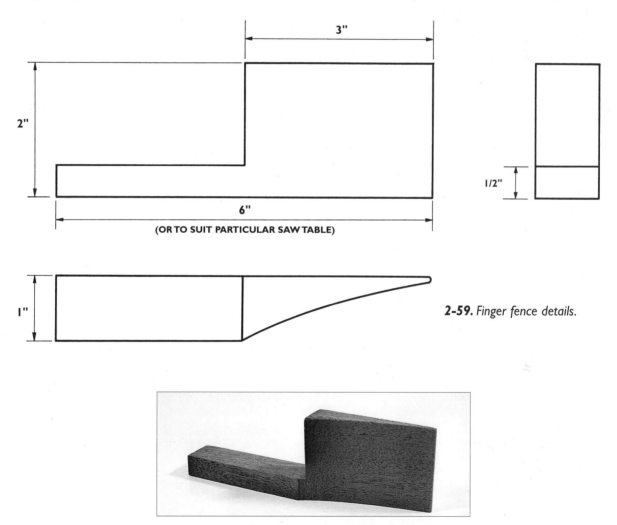

3"

2"

6"

(OR TO SUIT PARTICULAR SAW TABLE)

1/2"

1"

2-59. Finger fence details.

2-60. For parallel curved work, a finger fence is practical. This one is user-made and cut from an odd piece of hardwood.

USING A FINGER FENCE

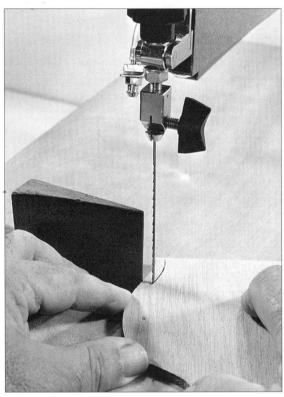

2-61. *Having established the required curve cut accurately freehand, set up the fence at the required width to suit the workpiece. A test run is advisable to ascertain that the cut runs freely without strain on the blade.*

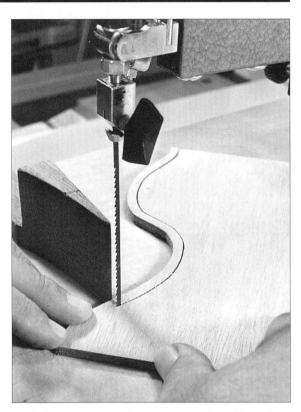

2-62. *All should be well if the point of the "finger" on the fence is exactly aligned with the blade teeth at right angles to the line of travel.*

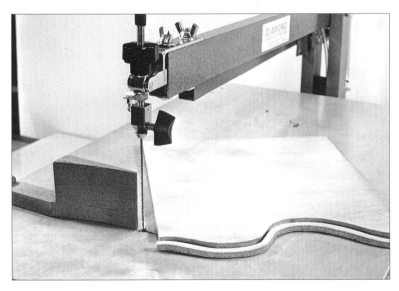

2-63. *Once set, parallel strips can be sawn at any profile at the prescribed width.*

CIRCLE-CUTTING JIG

When cutting circles, it is possible to scribe a circle with a pair of compasses and saw it freehand. It is also possible, but not recommended, to place a panel pin in the center of a workpiece and tap it into the worktable (providing it is of wood, of course). The pin then acts as a pivot, permitting a circle to be cut as it is rotated (2-64). I have seen this done, successfully and repeatedly, at a craft show by a fellow cutting out table mats, in a stack, several at a time.

A more sophisticated way is to cut circles with a jig made for the job, by Diamond (2-65). It requires a hole to be drilled into the rear of the worktable, to accept the fixing screw of the base of the jig (2-66). The arm that is attached to the base carries a point, adjustable for height, to suit

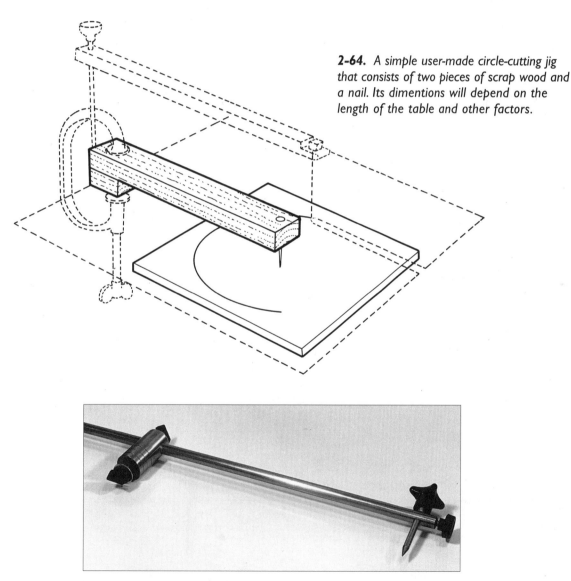

2-64. *A simple user-made circle-cutting jig that consists of two pieces of scrap wood and a nail. Its dimentions will depend on the length of the table and other factors.*

2-65. *The Diamond circle-cutting jig, complete and ready for fitting.*

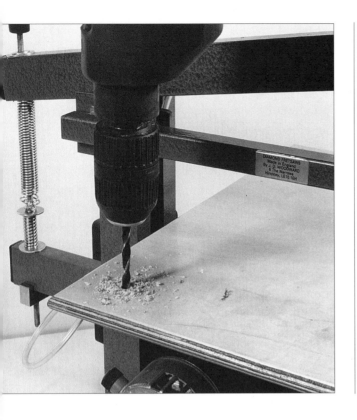

different workpieces of different thicknesses. When the point is utilized in the proposed circle center, it acts as a pivot. Positioning of the arm is crucial for accurate circle-cutting, and several trials are recommended to ascertain the production of perfect circles. This usually requires adjustment of the point towards or away from the base, at the relevant distance from the blade. Once set, the circle-cutting jig will saw circles reliably (2-67 and 2-68).

Refer to Cutting Circles on pages 114 and 115 for more information on cutting circles.

2-66 (left). A hole is drilled in the worktable to accommodate the pillar-fixing bolt.

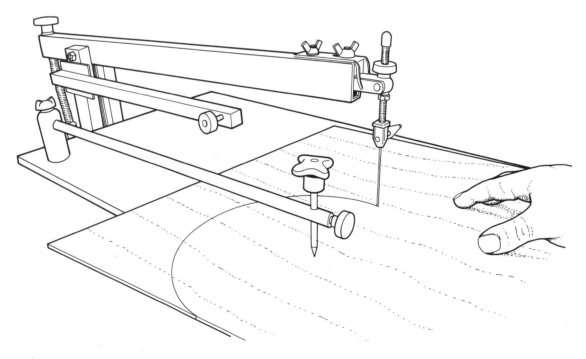

2-67. A commercially available circle-cutting accessory attachable by a screw through a hole drilled into the table. It is important to position the pivot point at the correct width and distance from the table. See 2-68.

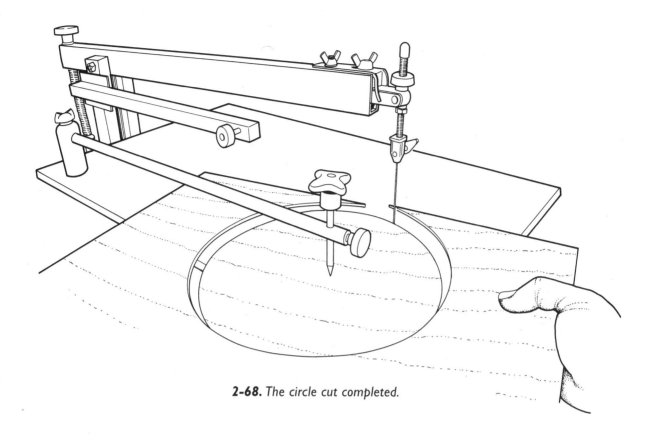

2-68. The circle cut completed.

ANCILLARY TABLE

Occasionally, if cutting pieces smaller than the hole in the worktable or insert through which the blade passes, there is the need to provide a special worktable.

Normally, the hole in the worktable is large enough for the blade to pass through it both in its upright position and at an angle. This clearance is often too large to support small workpieces. There is the risk of losing or jamming the workpiece in the hole and damaging it, the table, or fingers, and maybe even breaking the blade. One solution is to make an ancillary table with a smaller blade hole for temporary use. Ancillary tables are used on band saws and circular saws for similar reasons.

Any rigid board can be used for an ancillary table, but it should be no thicker than necessary to ensure stability, because it reduces arm clearance (2-69 to 2-71). Plastic-faced boards are ideal, because they are rigid and have a smooth, level surface.

Since it should fit the worktable, the ancillary table needs to be secure. Clamps can't be used because they will impede the movement of the workpiece, so it is best to cut the ancillary table sufficiently large to fit blocks around its periphery for quick and positive positioning. Care must be taken to pierce the blade hole accurately in the ancillary table to prevent unwanted contact with the blade (2-72 to 2-75). A useful guide would be to take precise measurements of the mounted blade relative to the standard table.

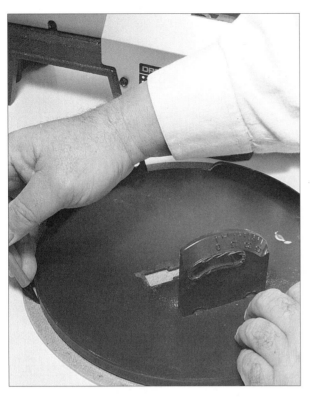

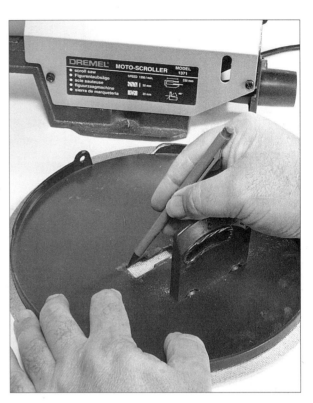

2-69 (left). *If the hole in the table is too big to support small workpieces, it may be necessary to make an ancillary table with a smaller blade hole. To make an ancillary table, in this case a circular one, cut a blank from a thin board. It should be sufficiently bigger than the original table to permit the placing of spacers around its perimeter. Here the table diameter is being marked on the blank.* **2-70 (right).** *Marking the blade hole is important to ensure accurate placement of the blade.*

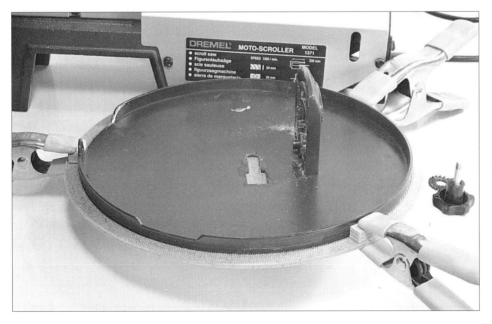

2-71. *Spacing lugs are attached with adhesive. These will allow quick positioning of the ancillary table to the worktable and prevent it slipping.*

2-72. *Measure carefully the position of the blade relative to the hole.*

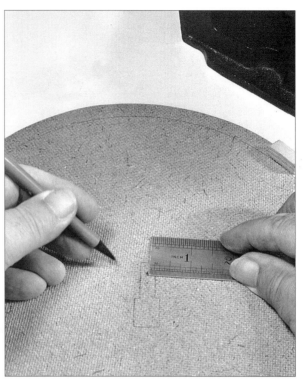

2-73. *The blade position is marked accurately on the ancillary table.*

2-74. *Using an Archimedean drill to pierce the blade hole.*

2-75. *The ancillary table ready for use. It has a tight blade hole that supports the piece all around it, and is especially suitable for small pieces.*

CHAPTER **3** Saw Blades

Blade-Selection Guidelines

The blade is the most crucial component in the whole scroll-sawing setup. It is impossible to overstress the importance of using the correct blade in a specific woodworking situation!

Four factors that should be considered when determining the proper blade to use are: 1, the kind of material being cut; 2, the hardness of the material; 3, the thickness of the material; and 4, whether the sawing operation is level or at an angle and straight or curved. Refer to Chapter 5 for a description of the cutting characteristics of the different types of material, to get an understanding of their characteristics, including their hardness and thickness.

Remember, there is no such thing as an average all-purpose blade if best results are required. It is, however, possible to limit the number of general-purpose blades to as few as six or seven, but experimentation is essential to establish what is best for individual requirements.

Saw blades are relatively inexpensive, so select a wide range of different types and sizes. Make trial cuts on different materials, carefully recording the data. This allows scroll-saw users to become knowledgeable, not only on the subject of blade-grading, but also on their own scroll saw

and its ability to cut different types of materials.

Some scroll-saw users mistakenly choose a packet of saw blades merely because of their grade numbers, sometimes on the advice of so-called "experts." This grading system is based on the Universal Generic Numbering (U.G.N) system, which is an attempt to standardize saw blades. Unfortunately, not all manufacturers follow the principles inherent in this system. One reason this system is not successful is because it does not include parameters for tooth design and gullet size.

There are 14 different grades of blades in the U.G.N. system. The first grade, 2/0, refers to the finest blade in the numbering system, which is .010 inch thick by .020 inch wide, with 28 teeth per inch (t.p.i.). The coarsest blade, the No. 12 grade, is .023 thick by .070 wide, and has 17 teeth per inch. Table 3-2 on page 69 includes the U.G.N. system for different blades and their corresponding dimensions. Note that it does not take into account the blade's tooth design, gullet design, etc. (3-1 and 3-2).

There are two guidelines that will help scroll-saw users select a blade. First, remember to use a finer blade for thinner material. Second, number 1,3,5,7, and 9 blades as described in the U.G.N. system should help scroll-sawyers cope with most cutting applications. Refer to Table 3-4 on page 71 for more information.

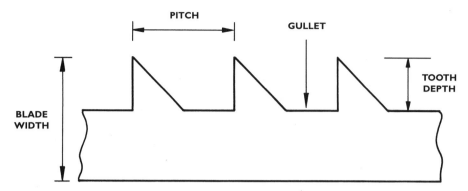

3-1. *Parts and characteristics of a scroll-saw blade. Pitch is the distance between the teeth of a saw blade. Gullet is the depth and form of the gaps between the teeth of a blade. Tooth depth is the distance between the point of the tooth and the bottom of the gullet. This is the thickness of the material removable, theoretically, by each tooth, each stroke. Blade width is the actual width of the material from which the blade is made, usually greater than its thickness. Blade thickness is the actual thickness of material from which the blade is made.*

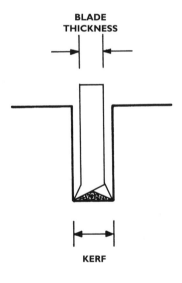

3-2. *A saw cut is referred to as a kerf. The wider the kerf relative to the thickness of the blade, the less friction is produced and the smaller the manageable radius.*

TABLE 3-1

	Teeth Per Inch	Thickness (Inch)	Width (Inch)
A	10	.015	.041
B	11.5	.017	.048
C	12	.015	.046
D	15	.016	.042

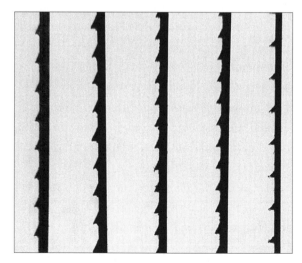

3-3. *Note the differences in the tooth designs of these blades, all of which are called No. 7 blades.*

Selecting blades on the basis of the numbering system alone presents some interesting results. Table 3-1 indicates the characteristics of No. 7 blades bought from four different suppliers. No. 7 blades with different tooth designs are also shown in 3-3.

Now, let us suppose it is desirable to choose our blade by the number of teeth per inch.

TABLE 3-2   **Universal Generic Numbering System**

Universal Generic No.	Teeth per inch	Thickness (inch)	Width (inch)
2/0	28	.010	.022
0	25	.011	.024
1	23	.011	.025
2	20	.012	.029
3	18	.013	.032
4	15	.014	.033
5	14	.015	.037
6	13	.016	.040
7	12	.016	.043
8	11.5	.017	.04
9	11.5	.018	.05
10	11	.019	.059
11	9.5	.019	.063
12	9.5	.020	.067

Unfortunately, suppliers rarely include this rather important information on their packages. Only close examination with a magnifying lens will provide the answer.

Let's assume we have now selected only blades with 14 teeth per inch (3-4). Table 3-3 shows four blades, all of which have 14 teeth per inch. Note the differences in their widths and thicknesses.

TABLE 3-3

	Grade No.	Thickness (Inch)	Width (Inch)
A	12	.023	.063
B	12	.025	.0460
C	9	.016	.041
D	7	.026	.087

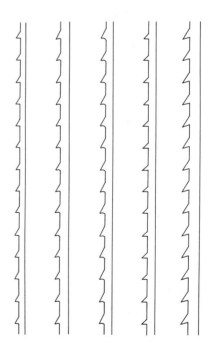

3-4. These blades all have the same pitch, 14 t.p.i. Compare the tooth profiles, the difference in proportion between the tooth depth and the blade stock.

BLADE-SELECTION GUIDLINES

When selecting a blade, remember the following:

1. The four major factors in determining which blade to use are the kind of material being cut, the thickness of the material, the hardness of the material, and whether cutting level or at an angle and straight or curved.

2. A selection of 6-10 general-purpose blades should be adequate.

3. Keep as wide a selection as possible of different types and sizes of blades. Number 1, 3, 5, 7, and 9 blades in the Universal Generic Numbering system should prove helpful in most cutting applications.

4. Experimentation is the key to determining how different grades of blades work on various types of material (3-5 to 3-8).

5. As a general rule, use finer blades for thinner materials.

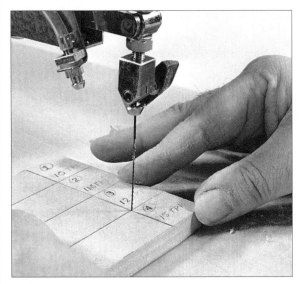

3-5. A simple test using four No. 7 blades from four different manufacturers. Each cut a kerf 1 inch across a medium-density-fiberboard workpiece, 1/2-inch thick. The first blade has 10 teeth per inch, the second 11.5, the third 12, and the fourth 15. All were run at about 1,000 spm (strokes per minute) at a uniform feed.

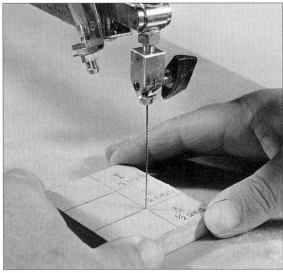

3-7. Making additional tests with the fourth blade used in 3-5 and 3-6. Here, a three-inch-wide workpiece is set up and marked to be cut in three equal sections. For the first section, the blade will be used at 175 spm (strokes per minute); for the second, at 370 spm; and for the third, at 700.

3-6. All four blades gave an acceptable finish on the cut face. There was slightly less tear-out at the bottom of the cut made by the fourth blade. That blade was also the easiest to steer.

3-8. Predictably, the blade used at 700 spm on the third section was the most satisfactory in terms of the smoothness of the cut surface and the cutting speed, but it was not easy to steer. Almost no bottom breakout occurred.

Material Type	1/16 inch or less	1/8 inch	1/4 inch	1/2 inch	3/4 inch	1 inch or more	Speed Range
Aluminum*	0**	1	2				300/60
Bone, Ivory	4	5	6				700/1500
Brass*	3/0	2/0	0				200/400
Card, Paper	5	6					700/1500
Felt	6	8	10	12			500/1000
MDF	4	5	6	8	10	12	700/1500
Particleboard	5	7	9	10	11	12	700/1500
Plastics (Hard)	4	5	6	8			200/500
Plastics (Soft)	6	8	9	10			150/300
Plywood	4	5	6	8	10	12	700/1500
Rubber	6	8	10				200/400
Steel*	4/0	3/0	2/0				200/400
Wood (Hard)	4	5	6	8	10	12	700/1500
Wood (Soft)	1	3	5	7	8	9	700/1500

*The blades used to cut metal are designed specifically for that purpose
**Indicates Universal Generic blade number.

Table 3-4. *This table shows the blades in the Universal Generic Numbering system recommended for cutting various types of material at different thickness, and the speed range at which they should be used. If a particular material is not shown in the chart, choose one of a similar kind for reference. If the area under a specific thickness is blank, this indicates that it is recommended that the material not be cut at that thickness, at least not without great caution. The information presented in this table should not be regarded as rigid. Remember, successful sawing operations depend greatly on balancing the type of blade with speed of reciprocation and feed rate.*

Basic Blade Information

The teeth of some scroll-saw blades bend outward from the blade shank (3-9). Usually, where blades are made this way, alternate teeth are bent away from each other. This is referred to as set. Not all blades have a "set" to their teeth. In fact, it depends greatly upon the production process as to whether or not the manufacturer can supply such a feature.

It is an easy matter to determine the extent of the set if there is access to simple calipers or a dial indicator (3-10 and 3-11). Measure the thickness at the end of the blade and compare it to the

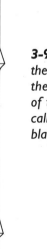

3-9. *The distance that the teeth are bent from the normal thickness of the blade body is called the "set" of the blade.*

thickness across the tooth points. There may be as much as 60 percent greater thickness across the teeth than across the end of the blade. An obvious advantage is that with the teeth cutting a slot or "kerf" wider than the blade body, there is no blade drag, friction is reduced, and it is easier for the blade to navigate curves.

Blade Length. Most standard blades are 5¼ to 5½ inches long. In fact, many woodworkers believe that blades are available in just these sizes. Even manufacturers do not list the length of the blades on the information on the packets, obviously because they also believe no other size will be suitable. Well, this is true enough in most cases, but on machines like the Diamond scroll saws it is possible to use blades up to 11 inches long. Such machines allow a greater-than-normal range of blade design, including heavy-duty blades similar to band-saw and hacksaw blades.

Kerf. A kerf is a cut made by the blade. The wider the kerf relative to the thickness of the blade, the less friction produced.

Pitch. The distance between the teeth on a blade is known as pitch. In comparative terms, when the distance is short, the blade is considered fine. When the distance is long, the blade is considered coarse.

DETERMINING BLADE SET

3-10. Measuring the thickness of the blade body using vernier calipers with a dial indicator. The blade is .019 inch thick.

3-11. When the calipers are used to measure across the teeth of the same blade to determine the "set" of the teeth, they measure .028 inch.

Blade Types

There are two distinct types of scroll-saw blades: pin- and plain-end blades. Pin-end blades are available in a limited range of relatively coarse, wide sizes. The reason for the restricted size range is due to the fact that the cross-pins are fitted into holes punched into the ends of the blade. Obviously, there is a limit to how small a cut can be made with these blades.

Plain-ended blades are available in just about every size and type. These include wood- and metal-cutting blades, as well as spiral and skip- and reverse-tooth blades (3-12).

Suppliers will not have every type and size of blade in stock, so some shopping around might be necessary to find particular blades.

STANDARD WOOD-CUTTING BLADES

Wood-cutting blades have a basic form (3-13). They generally have deep gullets. Provided the machine is adjustable for holding blades of different lengths, it may be possible to use longer

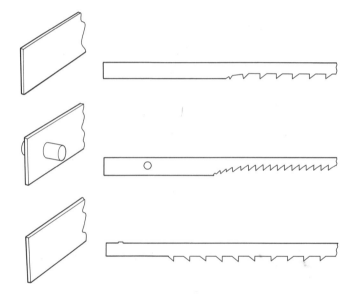

3-12. Three different types of blades. At top is a plain-end blade with a skip-tooth pattern. In the middle is a pin-end blade with fine, regular teeth. On the bottom is a plain-end reverse-tooth blade. The bottom six teeth of the plain-end reverse-tooth blade point upward, to help cleanly cut the bottom edge of the workpiece.

3-13. An enlarged view of deep-gullet blades for sawing thick wooden stock. The narrower ones are for profile work. The blades, from left to right, are as follow: a 3/16-inch-wide blade with 6 teeth per inch (tpi); a 3/16-inch blade with 4 tpi; a 1/4-inch blade with 6 tpi; a 1/4-inch blade with 4 tpi; a 3/8-inch blade with 6 tpi; and a 1/2-inch blade with 6 tpi. These blades were made from band-saw blades.

CUTTING THICK WOOD

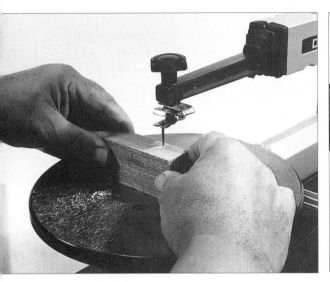

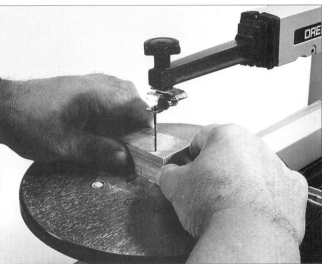

3-14. *Two-inch-thick hardwood proved almost impossible to cut with a regular pin-end No. 7 blade on this scroll saw with a 1/4-inch stroke. The blade cannot clear the sawdust because its stroke is too short to cut wood this thick.*

3-15. *The same blade cutting 1-inch-thick wood at the same speed, satisfactorily. The scroll saw used is a basic single-speed C-frame scroll saw.*

blades than standard when cutting thicker materials (3-14 and 3-15).

METAL-CUTTING BLADES

Many soft metals like aluminum, soft brass, and steel may be sawn satisfactorily with standard wood-cutting blades, but for hard metals it is best to use those made specially for the job (3-16). Jewelers' blades, for instance, are intended, as the name implies, for fine metal work, including precious metals such as gold and silver. These are fine-toothed narrow blades that have virtually no set.

SKIP-TOOTH BLADES

Most scroll-saw blades have a skip-tooth design in which every other tooth is missing (3-17).

3-16. *Metal-cutting blades of various widths and teeth per inch. The blades are, from left to right: a 1/16-inch-wide blade with 24 tpi; a 1/8-inch blade with 24 tpi; a 3/16-inch blade with 14 tpi; a 1/4-inch blade with 14 tpi; a 3/8-inch blade with 14 tpi; and a 1/2-inch blade with 14 tpi.*

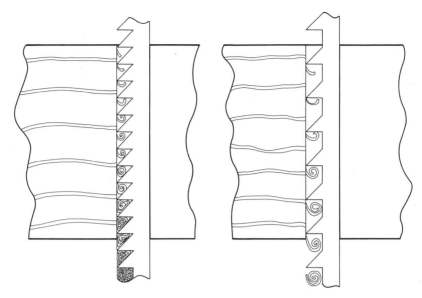

3-17. Cross-sectional views of two blades. The blade on the left cannot work efficiently because its teeth have become blocked with wood shavings. In this situation, the blade is likely to burn due to excessive friction, damaging itself and the workpiece. The skip-tooth blade on the right has room to cut waste and push it through the kerf, eliminating any blockage, until the chips are ejected at the bottom.

This creates a gap equal to a whole tooth between the teeth points. On some blades, this gap, or gullet, is even greater. A further variation on this design is the double skip-tooth bladeswhich has teeth grouped in pairs with a double gap between.

REVERSE-TOOTH BLADES

This confusing title is given to a blade made with about half a dozen teeth at the bottom of the blade pointing upwards, rather than downwards (refer again to 3-12). Normally, the bottom edge of a sawn workpiece may become slightly ragged from the blade teeth. With reverse-tooth blades, this doesn't occur because the teeth that point upwards remove most the ragged edge on the return stroke. When these blades are used, there may be an increased tendency to lift the workpiece on the upstroke, but it is not excessive enough to create a great problem and a hold-down can also be used if need be.

SPIRAL BLADES

A spiral blade is one that has been twisted to produce a cutting edge all around it (3-18). It has fairly coarse teeth that produce a rough surface finish on the cut face of the workpiece (3-19). However, it is possible to cut on all sides of the blade, achieving the possibility of moving the workpiece in any direction radially, relative to the blade, without the need to rotate it. This type of blade works very well on an inclined worktable when it may be difficult to rotate some workpieces.

Refer to Sawing with a Spiral Blade on pages 137 to 140 for more information on spiral blades.

3-18. A spiral blade. Note that teeth are arranged all around the blade. This allows for multi-directional cutting with-out the need to rotate the workpiece.

3-19. Two spiral blades. The one on the left, the smaller one, is a No. 1 blade. The one on the right is a No. 7 blade. They can be used to cut in any direction with a fairly fast stroke to allow for a relatively coarse blade profile.

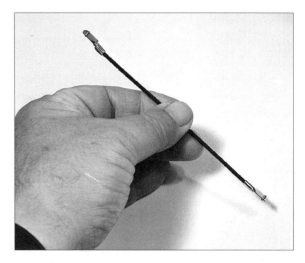

3-20. An abrasive rod used to cut hard materials and suitable for cutting stone, ceramics, glass, etc. It is recommended that relatively slow speeds be used with this tool.

ABRASIVE-COATED RODS

There are also abrasive-coated rods available which have flattened, cross-pinned ends (3-20). They fit into conventional, pin-type blade holders, and are tensioned in the same way as regular blades. They are very useful for cutting ceramics, metals, stone, glass, and other hard materials. Durable and economical, they are great assets to scroll-sawyers who want to use their machines as fully as possible.

Improving Blades

ROUNDING BLADE BACKS

In the distant past, blades came with smooth, rounded backs, making it easier for the blade to negotiate the workpiece. Due primarily to contemporary production methods, current blades do not have rounded backs. This makes it easier for the manufacturer to make the blade, rather than benefiting the customer.

Scroll-sawyers can easily round the back of

scroll-saw blades with a piece of Carborundum stone or maybe a piece of broken sharpening hone. After mounting the new blade in the scroll saw and setting the blade speed, hold the stone against the back of the blade, and move it around, taking off the sharp corners and generally smoothing the surface (3-21).

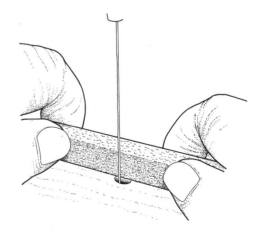

3-21. To remove sharp corners on the back of a blade, a small abrasive stone is applied while the scroll saw is activated.

REMOVING BURRS

Some methods of blade production produce a burr on one side of the blade. Although it is almost intangible to the touch and invisible to the naked eye, it causes the blade to track slightly to one side during the cut.

It is possible to use a technique similar to the one used to round blade backs to remove a slight burr. This requires a steady, sensitive touch and a very fine abrasive, in order to remove the burr without destroying the profile of the teeth. Applied correctly, this technique can improve the performance of the blade and refine the forward tracking of the workpiece when it is following the sawing line.

MODIFYING THE CROSS-PINS ON PIN-END BLADES

If it is necessary to use pin-end blades to cut holes, it might be that the cross-pins are larger than the entry holes. This can be corrected by reducing the length of the cross-pins with the use of a powered grindstone. An alternative method would be to use a Carborundum stone to grind them down to size (3-22). If doing this, remember that the pins must not be shortened to less than the gap width of the blade holder.

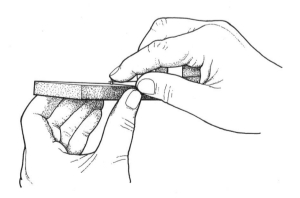

3-22. *Using a Carborundum stone to grind cross-pins.*

MODIFYING THE WIDTHS OF PIN-END BLADES

The width of the ends of some pin-end blades, that is, the distance from the point of the tooth to the back of the blade, is often greater than the width of the blade itself. Again, this excess can be ground away using the same methods as suggested for shortening pins.

CUTTING WORKPIECES LONGER THAN THE THROAT DEPTH

Few scroll saws have the facility to swivel blade holders, although blade holders can be attached at right angles. Swiveling blade holders become necessary when cutting workpieces longer than the throat depth, or in other words, if the rear frame obstructs the passing of the workpiece. One way to resolve this problem is to twist the ends of the blade to the desired angle so that when the blade is installed in the blade holder, its teeth face to the side rather than to the front (3-23 and 3-24). It is then a simple matter to feed the material across the scroll saw for the sawing operation. This method could theoretically cope with a workpiece of limitless length.

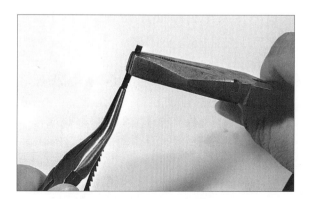

3-23. *Twisting blade ends to permit the passing of workpieces sideways across the worktable. This allows a board of limitless length to be sawn.*

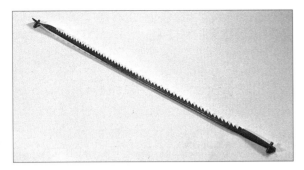

3-24. A pin-end blade with twisted ends. It is important to make the two ends parallel to each other and at right angles to the blade stock.

Blade Holders

If the saw blade is the most crucial component in the scroll saw, then for sure the blade holder (often referred to as a blade clamp) is next in importance. If the blade holder is inefficient or difficult to use, life can become very frustrating for the sawyer. Blade holders, no matter what their design, are clamped to the blade ends to hold them in place. Whether this clamping action is achieved by squeezing together two sides of a vise-type holder, closing one side of a holder against another with the blade in between, or by bringing the end of a screw against the blade to force it against the side of the holder, all methods will work to one degree or another.

There are many different types of blade clamps and blade-suspension systems. The most basic systems are used for pin-end scroll-saw blades (3 25 to 3-29). Some can be used for both pin- and plain-end blades (3-30 to 3-34). Variations include V-shaped holders (3-35 to 3-38); holders with pivot bars (3-39); split-blade holders that use a turn key to tighten the clamping screw (3-40); stirrup-type holders (3-41 to 3-46); swiveling blade holders (3-47 to 3-54); and quick-acting blade holders (3-55 to 3-59). Sometimes jigs and accessories help facilitate blade-changing (3-60 to 3-69).

There is little that can be done to improve the holder as supplied with the machine, except to change it if it is completely wrong for the planned work. As an example, take the projects that involve sawing inside openings. With this type of work, holes have to be drilled into the workpiece. If the holder is large, the blade has to be taken off the scroll saw to fit it in the blade holder after it is inserted into the workpiece. This is clumsy and time consuming, and is likely to lead to accidents of one kind or another. It is better to change the holder for a type that allows for easier insertion of the blade, or better still, one that permits the insertion of the blade without the need to remove it from the machine. Many manufacturers offer alternative holders. These products have usually been upgraded over the years. This is an indication of a perceptive and supplier who recognizes the need for improvement.

BLADE-HOLDING-SYSTEM GUIDELINES

1. Look for a blade-holding system with the following characteristics: A, a minimal blade-loading and unloading movement; B, a means of readily connecting it to the tensioning device; C, ready access to the partially detached blade, for insertion into holes for internal-sawing.

2. Experiment with different holders. This is another situation in which experimentation will pay dividends. Many different types of scroll saws (and blade holders) can be found at the countless woodworking, crafts, and model-making exhibitions that occur throughout the year.

3. It is helpful to have available two sets of holders if they are of the detachable kind. This allows different blades to be available for insertion into the machine if it is necessary to use more than one size or type when cutting different materials.

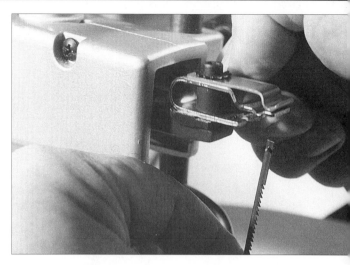

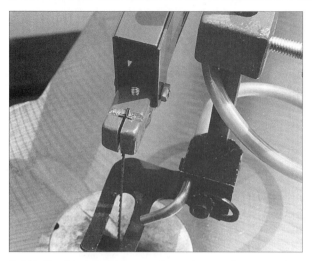

3-25. *This blade holder is perhaps the simplest one of them all. It has a vertical slot to accept pin-end blades. The groove across its top will hold the cross pins securely when tension is applied.*

3-27. *Pin-end blades are held in the slot in the lower portion of this blade holder. Above the holder is a spring jaw designed to hold stirrup-type holders for plain-end blades.*

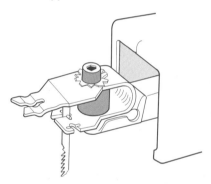

3-26. *A blade holder with dual-position slots. A standard pin-end blade is fitted in the forward- facing position. It can also be fitted into the adjacent slot, allowing it to face sideways to the teeth. If the blade is fitted in the latter position, long workpieces may be fed across the table. Above and forward of the slots is a groove to accept stirrup-type blade holders.*

3-28. *The cross-pin in the blade is lodged firmly in place in the groove formed for that purpose.*

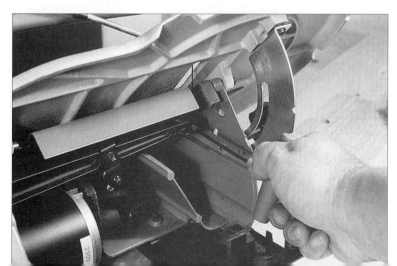

3-29. *Tightening the clamp when attaching the blade to the lower arm necessitates the use of a long-shank socket-type key. This is facilitated by the removal of the side cover. So often, scroll-saw casing is little more than a cosmetic obstruction.*

BLADE HOLDERS FOR PIN- AND PLAIN-END BLADES

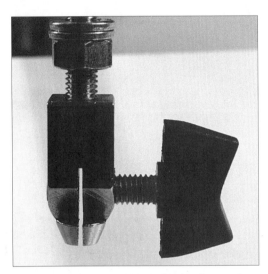

3-30. Another type of blade holder designed to accept either plain- or pin-end blades. This view shows the slot machined to receive plain-end blades. The blade is clamped to the holder with the screw that is conveniently wing-shaped.

3-31. This view of the blade holder shows the slot made to accept pin-end blades. The blade holder can be rotated without removing it from the machine.

3-32. The top and bottom holders on this scroll saw are fitted with a pin-end blade. The knurled hand screw on the top holder is for final tensioning. Note: the worktable has been removed.

BLADE HOLDERS FOR PIN- AND PLAIN-END BLADES (CONTINUED)

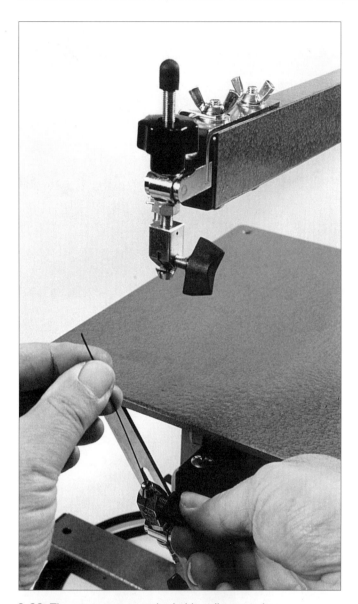

3-34. The same blade holder shown in 3-32 being used to hold a plain-end blade, without the need to change any parts.

3-33. The wing screws on the holder allow it to be manipulated as the blade is being clamped.

V-SHAPED BLADE HOLDERS

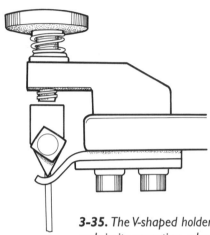

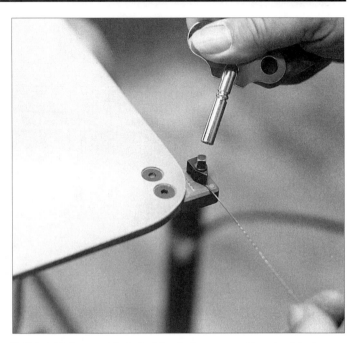

3-35. The V-shaped holder can rock in its mounting when the saw blade is subjected to pressure when sawing. This reduces the stress on the blade by allowing it to flex.

3-36. A V-shaped blade holder helps to position the blade visually while it is being clamped. The wing-shaped key is convenient and efficient.

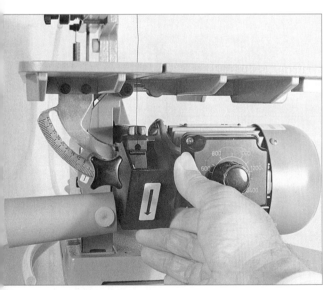

3-37. Access to the lower blade holder is made easier by lowering the hinged cover.

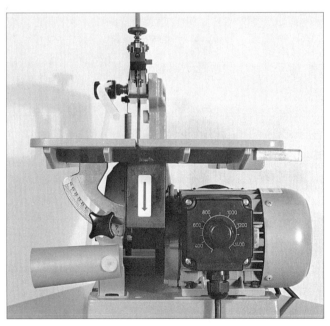

3-38. After the blade is installed, the cover is returned to conceal the lower blade clamp.

HOLDER WITH PIVOT BAR

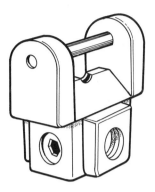

3-39. *This blade holder has a pivot bar that attaches to the cradle at the arm terminals. The socket screw is used to clamp the blade to the holder.*

SPLIT-BLADE HOLDER

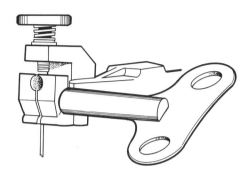

3-40. *A split blade holder that uses a turn key to tighten the clamping screw. The knurled screw on the top prevents the holder from detaching from the cradle.*

STIRRUP-TYPE HOLDERS

3-41. *A pair of stirrup-type holders. The grub screws can be inspected through the side hole of the blade to make certain that the blade is centered.*

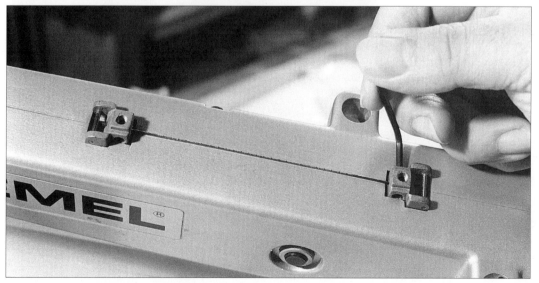

3-42. *A practical aid for blade location is provided by recessed pockets in the scroll saw's casing.*

3-43. If the holder screws are arranged correctly, the blade should be centered in the blade holder and ready for installation in the scroll saw.

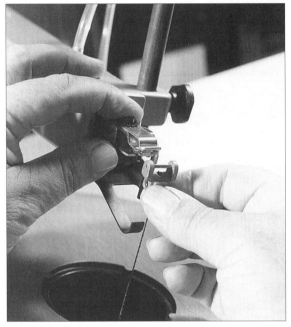

3-44. Attaching a blade to a stirrup-type blade holder is easy. It requires only a push to position it in the upper spring jaw.

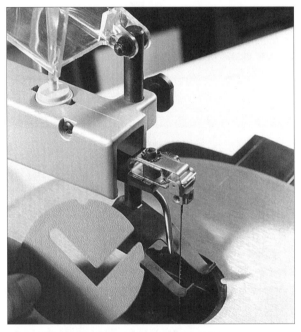

3-45. It is necessary to remove the table insert to get access to the lower blade holder because the stirrup blade holder is larger than the hole in the table insert.

3-46. When the table insert is removed, the lower blade holder can be seen. It is easier to attach blades to stirrup blade holders with the side cover removed, because this gives access for the hand below the table.

SWIVELING BLADE HOLDERS

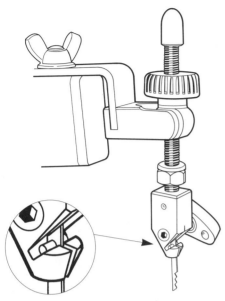

3-47. *This swivel clamp is holding a pin-end blade. The groove machined across the holder accepts and lodges the cross-pin. After fine tensioning, the lower lock nut is screwed upwards to prevent loosening.*

3-49. *Swiveling blade holders allow some ease of manipulation during blade installation, but more beneficial is the fact that they will move when the blade is under stress when sawing. This alleviates the strain on the blade.*

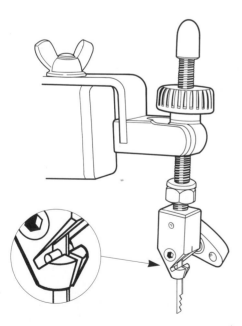

3-48. *This plain-end blade is located in the vertical slot of the swivel holder. It is attached to the swivel clamp by tightening the hand screw.*

3-50. *Note how much this upper blade holder swivels. The lower blade holder similarly.*

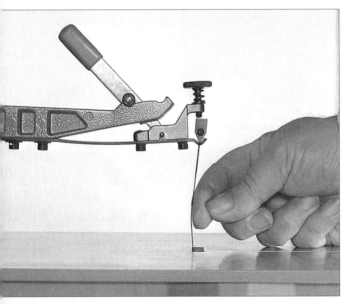

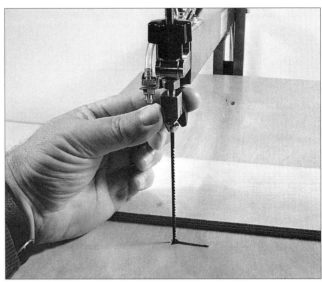

3-51. *Both blade holders swivel front and back to compensate for the deflection of the blade. Without this, the blade would be under much greater stress.*

3-53. *A similar swiveling function is available with this type of holder. Its V shape allows a rocking action when the blade is deflected under stress. Even with the blade under tension, it is possible to rotate the holders 360 degrees, a feature with several benefits.*

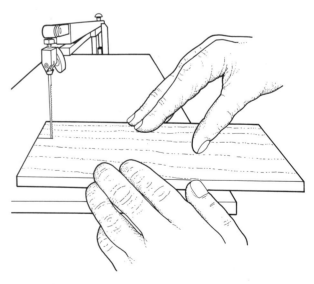

3-52. *It is normal for a scroll-saw blade to flex when under stress. Although this example is somewhat exaggerated, it nonetheless indicates that the swiveling action of this type of holder compensates greatly for blade deflection.*

3-54. *When swiveling blade holders are used, it is possible to cut a workpiece that is too long to pass between the blade and the rear frame by setting the blade at right angles and cutting across the table.*

QUICK-ACTING BLADE HOLDERS

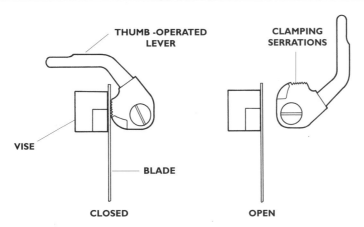

3-55. A quick-acting clamp. On the left, it is shown closed. On the right, it is shown open. In principle, it grips the blade more tightly the more tension is applied. In other words, the more effort that is applied to pull out the blade, the more tightly the serrated jaw holds it.

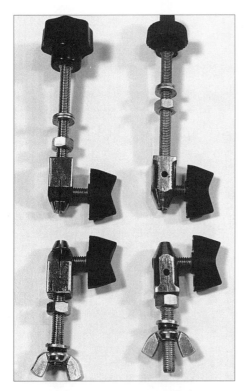

3-56. On the left are normal clamp-type holders with slots machined completely through them for blade access. On the right are quick-change holders, with holes drilled into their centers into which plain-end blades may be placed rapidly.

3-57. When fitted on the scroll saw, these holders have the same features as the standard ones, but have the added advantage of allowing blades to be changed rapidly.

QUICK-ACTING BLADE HOLDERS (CONTINUED)

3-58 (left). *Quick-change holders are advantageous when blades are being threaded into a workpiece. Blades can be attached to them quickly and accurately.*

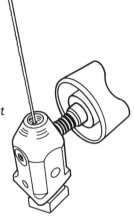

3-59 (right). *This super-fast blade holder is designed to be located by feel, since its central hole, being countersunk, effectively steers the blade into position so it is ready to be clamped by the action of the hand screw.*

BLADE-CHANGING JIGS AND ACCESSORIES

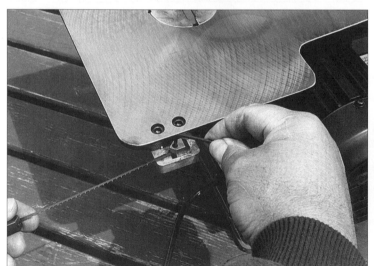

3-60. *It is easier to attach separate holders to blade ends when some form of clamping system is used. Shown here is a small jig with a pocket-like recess. The holder is placed into this recess, leaving the hands free to hold the blade and clamp the blade to the holder with a socket-like screw.*

3-61. *If the holder is fitted with a screw from either side, the screws must each be adjusted to center the holder. This applies to the bottom holder also; otherwise, the blade will not be vertical.*

BLADE-CHANGING JIGS AND ACCESSORIES (CONTINUED)

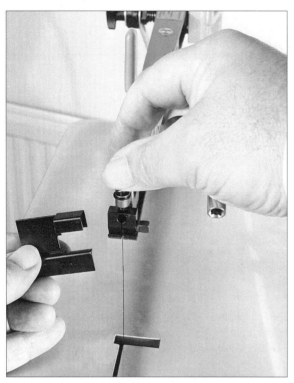

3-62. *Another method of changing blades quickly is achieved by attaching an accessory that locks the blade holder in place while the blade is being changed. Here it is shown being attached to the blade holder.*

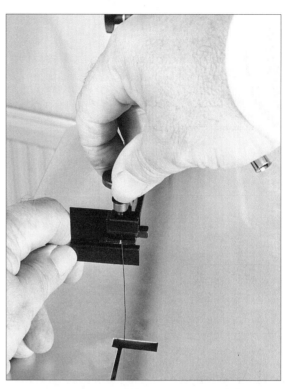

3-63. *The blade lock is slid onto the blade holder behind the blade. Pressure is exerted on the blade holder by tightening the upper screw, forcing the blade holder into the crook of the spring fork.*

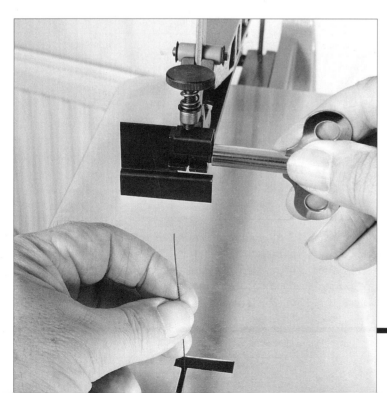

3-64. *With the holder fixed in place by the upper screw, tension can be reduced and the blade removed from the holder.*

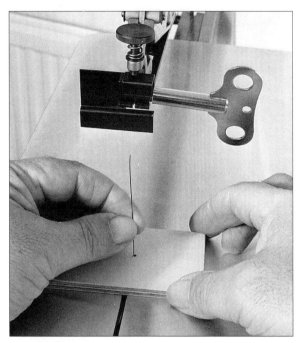

3-65. The blade is inserted into the workpiece, which has been prepared with a suitable hole.

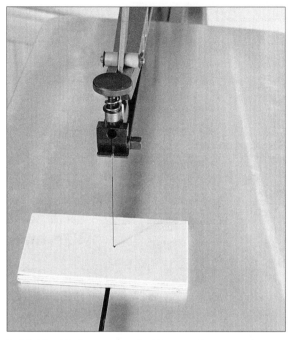

3-66. The blade is reinstalled by attaching it to the holder, tightening the clamp, and applying tension. The blade-locking device can then be removed, and the sawing begun.

3-67. This plastic knob is an accessory that can be used to replace the square-headed screw on the holder that required a key to clamp it, shown in 3-40.

3-68. An alternative to the plastic knob is a knurled metal knob. With this, the blade is clamped between two screws rather than squeezed by the clamp jaws. A grub screw is set to accommodate the width of the blade being used, leaving the knurled-head screw to control the clamping action.

3-69. Ready for sawing, the clamp can remain in the upper holder as a permanent feature if preferred. The over-center tensioning device is another feature that allows the blade to be quickly changed.

Adjustments and Tracking Procedures

RIGHT-ANGLE BLADE ADJUSTMENT

One of the fundamental requirements when using the scroll saw for general-purpose work is that the table be adjusted so that it is perfectly square or at right angles to the side of the blade. Some trial and error is inevitable when doing this, so a few pieces of scrap material are necessary.

The first step in ensuring that the table is perfectly square to, or at right angles to, the blade is by measurement. If the worktable has a protractor built into its tilt adjuster, set it at zero degrees (3-70). Then take a piece of wood with a flat bottom and cut it into two pieces. Inspect one of the parts with a try square. Note any angle deviation and adjust the angle (3-71). If the protractor/adjuster has a movable pointer, it may have to be adjusted to register precisely with the zero mark. Perseverance, an essential ingredient to

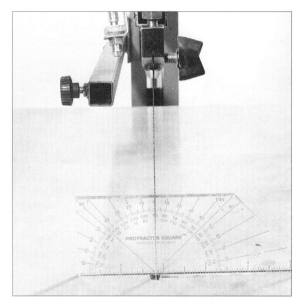

3-70. *Using a protractor for preliminary setting of the table for normal right-angle sawing.*

fine craftsmanship, is an advantage in this case.

There is another very simple, almost foolproof procedure that requires no extraneous equipment whatsoever. Take a scrap block close in size to the maximum thickness recommended for the

3-71. *The sawing angle is adjusted by inclining the worktable. A try square is being used to check the results of some test cuts.*

saw. Cut into the block no more than the thickness of the saw blade, and then withdraw the blade (3-72). Turn the block around to face the saw cut and place it behind the blade (3-73). Any deviation from a perfectly vertical cut will be doubled by this reversal. Adjust the table angle accordingly.

A set square can be checked in a similar way. Place the set square on a flat surface such as a bench top, with its stock against the front edge. Draw a line along the blade on the surface. Turn

3-72. *A simple, alternative method for checking that the blade is set square with the table. First, place a piece of wood with a known straight edge on the worktable. Then make a mark on it with the moving saw blade.*

3-73 (right). *Next, the test piece is turned round so that the saw mark faces the back of the blade. Any angular discrepancy will be apparent between the saw mark and the blade. Adjust the worktable angle if necessary.*

the square over so that the opposite side of the blade is in contact with the surface and make sure that the stock is firm against the front edge. If the square is set up at a true right angle, the blade edge should follow the pencil line.

SETTING BLADE ANGLES OTHER THAN 90 DEGREES

Let us consider the occasions when, for some reason, it becomes necessary to cut with the blade at other than a right angle to the worktable, such as when sawing bevels or miters. To set the table at the correct angle, first establish what the required angle is (3-74). Most worktables tilt by lowering the left side. Remember, this movement increases the angle between the left-hand side of the table and the blade, therefore decreasing the angle between the right-hand side of the table and the blade. This is important to remember when working with very small adjustments.

Even if the machine is fitted with a protractor on its adjustment device, it is advisable, as a matter of principle, to check the angle with the use of a transparent geometrical protractor before sawing (3-75), especially in cases in which the angle is critical, such as when matching joints in adjacent components.

After the angular sawing operation is complet-

3-74. *The protractor incorporated in the adjuster makes a good basic guide for setting the angle of the worktable when cutting bevels or miters. If precision is required, make test cuts by measuring the angle on the workpiece and fine-adjusting the table angle if necessary.*

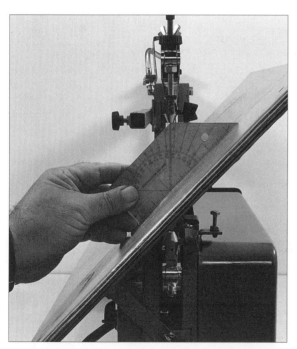

3-75. *A geometrical protractor, placed close to the blade for direct reading, may be used as an alternative to the protractor incorporated in the adjuster when checking the angle of the blade before sawing.*

ed, if it is necessary to return the table to its original position, check to see if the scroll saw is fitted with a "stop screw." With the stop screw, you can return the table to its former position without further adjustment (3-76).

3-76. *Under this worktable is a stop, with a lock nut, that allows the table to be set horizontally. This allows the operator to return the table to its normal angle after bevel-sawing without the need to adjust it.*

ADJUSTING FOR LONGER BLADES

The gap between the arms of certain scroll saws can be increased, which allows longer blades to be used. When the arms are spread, they are no longer parallel to each other. Therefore, it becomes necessary to adjust the blade holders to compensate for the altered position of the arms. It is not normally necessary to move the lower blade holder, but the upper one is moved out to extend the normal length of the arm. Some experimentation may be necessary if this is being tracked for the first time, but if a protractor is being used to compare the angles of the blade in its extreme positions, it should be easy to correctly adjust the blade holder (3-77 to 3-79).

STRAIGHT TRACKING

As mentioned in the previous sections, most blades have a tendency to drift to one side. This need not necessarily be a problem once the blade's movement or "bias" has been learned by the way it feels when sawing. Diamond scroll saws have blade holders that may be used to advantage in this respect. All of the blade holders used on these scroll saws, including the quick-change types, can be swiveled while under tension and without the need to change their tension (3-80).

Cutting the workpiece in a straight line rather than at a diagonal simply requires the rotation of the blade holder sufficiently to align it with the

3-77. *Using longer-than-normal blades requires more than simply raising the upper arm of the scroll saw to accommodate them. The upper blade holder has to be adjusted outwards to compensate for the altered geometry of the arms.*

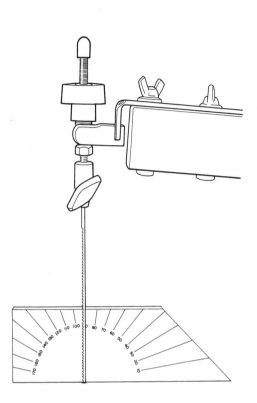

3-78. To ensure that the blade remains perfectly vertical after it has been adjusted, place a protractor on the table. At the lowest point of the arm stroke, the blade should be perpendicular to the table, as shown here.

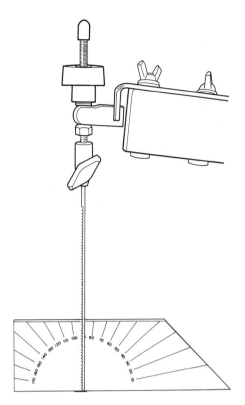

3-79. A secondary measurement, with the scroll-saw's arm stroke at its highest, reveals that the blade is still perpendicular, confirming that the upper carrier on the blade holder was accurately adjusted.

workpiece. An easy way to ascertain this realignment is to start a cut along a marked straight line, observing the degree to which the workpiece has to be angled in order to keep the blade on course (3-81). Then set the blade at a reciprocal angle by swiveling both blade holders and move the workpiece forward in a straight line (3-82).

3-80 (left). A refinement in blade-bias control is available with swiveling blade holders. Here a test piece is being sawn along a line drawn parallel to the sides

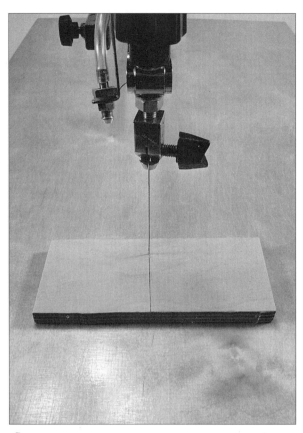

3-81. *To produce a straight cut that follows the kerf accurately, it is necessary to follow a diagonal path, being measured here by the protractor.*

3-82. *The blade holders are swiveled to the appropriate angle to compensate for the blade. Then cutting is resumed as the workpiece is moved forward in a straight line.*

4 Basic Sawing Principles and Techniques

Blades, Stroke Speed, and Feed Rate

Better Sawing Finesse is an entertaining mnemonic that can be used to remember the abbreviation B.S.F., which are the initials for blade, stroke, and feed. The Golden Rule in scroll-sawing is that the best way to ensure optimum cutting is by carefully balancing these three factors (4-1). Change one and the other two will be affected. Let's consider these three factors separately:

BLADES

In Chapter 2, it was shown that there is a wide variety of different types of blades. Regardless of which one is selected for a given job, its effectiveness will depend on its stroke speed and the rate at which the workpiece is fed towards the blade. When choosing a blade, consider the type of material being cut, including its thickness, and the kind of cut being made. This is probably a good time to refer to Table 3-4 on page 71, which recommends which blades to use in specific situations.

STROKE SPEED

Stroke speed is the speed at which the blade reciprocates. This is indicated as cutting strokes per minute (spm). Not all machines have variable speed. A standard one-speed machine probably has a high stroke speed and is not intended to be used to cut metals. Two- and three-speed models can be used to cut, to a certain extent, different materials or varying thickness, but it is the scroll saw with infinitely variable speeds that offers the most flexibility.

In general, hard materials require a slow stroke speed. If using a one-speed scroll saw, compensation for its high speed can be made by concentrating on using the correct blade and feed rate.

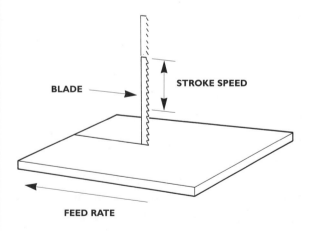

4-1. *Three factors that determine the effectiveness of the scroll saw are the type of blade used, its stroke speed, and the feed rate, the rate at which the operator feeds the material to the blade.*

FEED

Last but not least is the rate at which the blade is fed into the workpiece. Feed rate is basically governed by the operator's sense of touch. It is surprising how quickly it is possible to get a good feel for what is the correct feed rate, and many things contribute to assessing it. These include the pressure the workpiece exerts against the blade, the sound of the workpiece being cut, and the lower pitch of the motor under stress. Up to a point, it is best to aim for a rate of feed that produces as little pressure as possible on the blade, allowing it to remove the material without stress. On the other hand, if too slow a feed is imposed, there is a chance the workpiece will be burned and the blade damaged if it is too fine and applied to a thick, hard workpiece.

Hand Placement

Having taken the trouble, presumably, to determine which blade is correct for the required work and to set up the scroll saw properly for the scheduled tasks, the scroll-saw user next needs to consider two equally important components: the operator's hands! The hands are needed for two basic operations simultaneously: to hold down the workpiece, and to manipulate it relative to the saw blade (4-2 to 4-6). Disregarding for the moment small pieces of postage-stamp size or less, which demand special consideration, the workpiece may be held by a thumb and, at least, the forefinger of each hand. In most cases, the first and second fingers can be used in addition to the thumbs. The fingers should apply pressure vertically downwards to counteract the tendency for the blade to lift the

workpiece on the return stroke. This tendency may be greater than normal if a reverse tooth-blade is used. Reverse-tooth blades are described fully on page 75.

While the fingers are exerting downward pressure to prevent lifting of the workpiece, the thumbs should steer the workpiece, guiding the marked saw line towards the blade. It is essential to balance the downward pressure with lateral pressure to make a smooth cut.

CORRECT HAND PLACEMENT

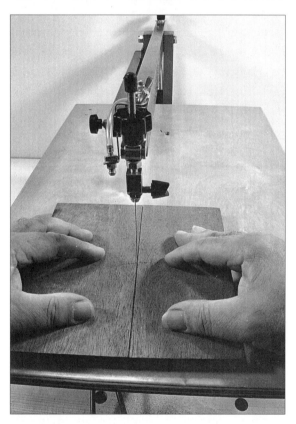

4-2. *The techniques for secure manipulation of the workpiece are the priority of the sawyer, beginning with the correct placement of the hands and fingers on the workpiece. The workpiece shown here has been partially sawn, and now the operator's fingers have to be repositioned for optimum support of the workpiece.*

4-3. *It is preferable to move one digit at a time to maintain downward pressure on the workpiece to prevent the possibility of the blade lifting the workpiece on the upstroke. Hands and fingers are moved continuously without halting the sawing operation. First step is to withdraw the right-hand index finger towards the thumb.*

4-4. *Now, move the middle finger of the right hand so that it follows the index finger.*

4-5. *The equivalent left-hand fingers are moved to match the right-hand fingers.*

4-6. *When all fingers have been repositioned, the thumbs and hands can be moved away from the blade. It is possible to maintain a continuous sequence of movement using this technique.*

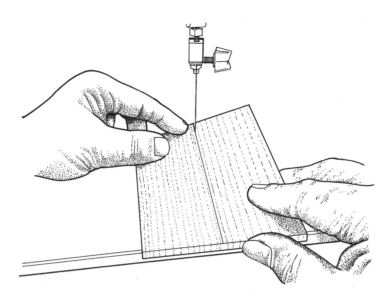

4-7. *If the workpiece is more than six inches wide, use one hand to hold down the workpiece and the other to steer it.*

CORRECT HAND TECHNIQUE

1. Use both hands to hold down and steer the workpiece.

2. Use at least one finger of each hand to provide hold-down pressure.

3. Use both thumbs for steering.

4. Place the digits safely behind or to the side of the blade whenever they are in proximity to it.

5. Apply the "walking" technique, that is, move one digit at a time, to relocate pressure on the workpiece.

6. Use thimbles for small work. Refer to Cutting Small Workpieces on pages 118 and 119 for more information. ■

Up to a point, the thumbs also help the fingers apply pressure downwards, particularly if they are placed on the edges of a workpiece thin enough to permit contact with its top as well as its edge. Symmetrical positioning of the digits on either side of the saw blade is suggested, for the sake of balance and security, wherever possible.

If the workpiece is wider than the space between the thumb and fingers, say more than six inches, the same positioning of the fingers should be applied provided that the workpiece does not exceed the length of the table between its front edge and the saw blade. If the workpiece is more than this width, it is recommended that the hands be separated. This means using one hand to hold down the workpiece, and the other one to steer it. In this case, with safety in mind, it is best to use one hand to hold down the workpiece with the fingers placed behind it and the thumb to the side of the blade, out of potential danger. Then steer the workpiece with the fingers and thumb of the other hand (4-7).

With small pieces about as big as a hand or smaller, only one hand position is needed without moving the digits once it has been placed on the workpiece until the completion of that sawing operation. In the case of a large workpiece, it will probably be necessary to reposition the digits to maintain correct pressure and control the steering. It is useful to contemplate the technique of the rock climber in this case. The rock climber moves only one limb at a time, in order to preserve the proper stance. In other words, move only one digit at a time. This requires a simple "walking" technique. Often, with larger pieces that cover most of the worktable, it is possible to place at least six digits (and sometimes all of them) on the workpiece, which puts sufficient downward pressure on the workpiece while it is being steered.

As mentioned earlier, exerting downward and lateral pressure on the workpiece is essential. Downward pressure has to be constantly applied. Any lessening of this pressure can lead to the blade lifting the workpiece. If this happens (one might say, "when this happens," because it is likely to happen to every beginner), the only way out of trouble is to switch off the scroll saw immediately. Here is where

the foot switch is of great value, permitting instant disconnection of the electrical supply. As was stated in Foot Switch on pages 22 and 25, a foot switch also allows the operator to place the hands in preparation for the sawing before switching on the machine.

As always, practice is the greatest long-term aid to ensuring good habits, provided it is accompanied by an awareness of correct procedures. Follow the short list of correct hand techniques on page 100 to help develop a secure technique. Now, spare a thought for my old friend Günther Kirsch, who, possessing the use of only one arm, not only managed to operate a scroll saw expertly, but also made his own machine!

Steering Techniques

WHAT ABOUT THE SAW LINE?

A line is marked on the workpiece before it is cut. This line, referred to as a saw line, indicates the path the blade should take when sawing the piece. Every time a cut is begun, and for its entire dura-

4-8. *Three sawn lines. The ones on the left and right show the procedure of leaving the line on one side or the other. As a general rule the line would be left so it can be used as a reference for determining the required size of the workpiece. The sawn line in the middle has been "split," leaving slight evidence of it on each side of the blade. A broader kerf from a thicker blade would have removed the line completely. Alternatively, a thinner mark would have been lost.*

tion, a decision has to be made as to whether to leave the line to one side of the blade, or to place the blade exactly on it and cut it away. In the case of a relatively thick line, it may be possible to "split" it, leaving a mark on either side of the cut (4-8).

The general rule concerning saw lines is to leave the line on a piece that is to be fitted to another part, in order to see that it is complete. If the line were sawn away, it would not be possible to see easily if the piece were undersize. In the case of components that need to fit together, it is better to split the line or to lose it completely in the kerf. It is a good principle to make a commitment to follow one technique, that is, to leave the line or to split it, and apply this technique once the cut has been started.

DEALING WITH BLADE BIAS

Allowance has to be made constantly for the tendency of the blade to cut more readily to one side than the other, often referred to as the blade's bias. Some random sawing on a piece of scrap will assist in getting the measure of how the blade cuts and the feel of its bias. Progressing to the stage where its bias can be reliably assessed is useful. For this, there is a simple exercise to develop the steering skills. Take a piece of scrap board and inscribe some straight lines about an inch or so in length at right angles to its edge along one side. Use these lines to practice sawing with the intention of leaving the lines, sometimes sawing to the left or right of the lines, and sometimes splitting them.

ON-THE-SPOT TURNS

Assuming that the "finger-walking" technique discussed on pages 100 and 101 have been practiced well enough to have become a good habit, the next useful skill to develop is on-the-spot turns. On-the-spot turns consist of spinning the workpiece 180 degrees around the blade. The ability to make on-the-spot turns allows the scroll-saw user to saw sharp inside or outside corners nonstop.

Medium-density fiberboard or particleboard will do for this exercise. To practice an on-the-spot turn, saw along a straight line for about an inch into a board, turn the board around 180 degrees, and move the blade out, leaving a clean slot. The objective is to leave as little as possible in the way of evidence that the workpiece has been turned around the blade. Since the blade is always wider than it is thick, it

4-9. On-the-spot turns consist of spinning the workpiece around 180 degrees on the blade. The object is to enter the blade into the workpiece for a short distance and then to rotate the workpiece around the blade with as little blade contact as possible.

must make a gap wider than the kerf on the on-the-spot turn. The hole created by the blade during the rotation of the workpiece is referred to as the "spin gap."

Follow these procedures for making an on-the-spot turn:

1. Cut along the saw line (4-9).

2. When the end of the line is reached, ease back just enough to remove pressure from the blade.

3. Ease the workpiece to the left. (Either side will do, but in this case, ease the workpiece toward the left.) The movement is minuscule, just enough to make the slightest contact with the right side of the blade.

4. Maintaining this light pressure on the side of the blade, rotate the workpiece counterclockwise, avoiding, as much as possible, contact with the blade teeth. Concentrate on maintaining contact with the "safe" sides of the blade (4-10). Continue this rotation gradually until the back of the blade

is bearing against the uncut end of the saw slot.

5. Have completed the 180-degree turn, withdraw the workpiece from the saw blade with as little contact as possible (4-11).

This whole sequence can be done in one smooth movement with a little practice, resulting in a trouble-free operation that removes the workpiece from the blade or leaves the blade ready to continue along another saw line. In time, on-the-spot turns can be made very quickly, increasing efficiency and, due to less exposure to error keeping the clearance gap at the end of the cut as small as possible.

Making On-the-Spot Turns with Various Blades

Use the previous exercise as a means of making on-the-spot turns with different blades to test them. It is not only a useful practice in itself, it also provides information about the kerf and the "spin gap" of different blades (4-12).

It will be discovered that it is possible to make

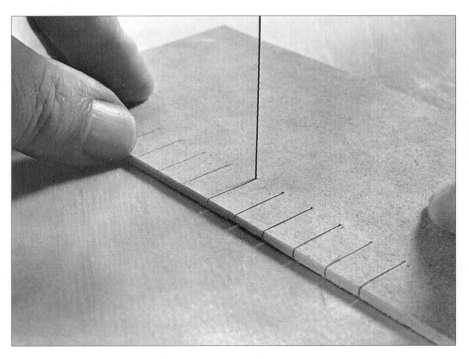

4-10. Here the workpiece has been rotated 180 degrees. The smooth back and sides of the blade bear safely against the saw slot.

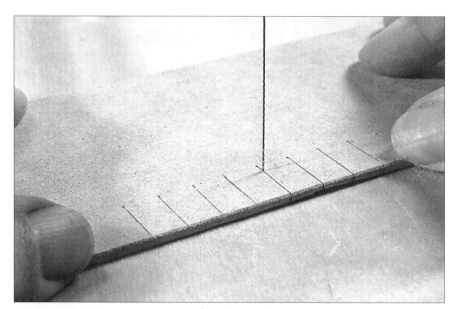

4-11. Now the workpiece is withdrawn, and there is little contact between the blade and the kerf.

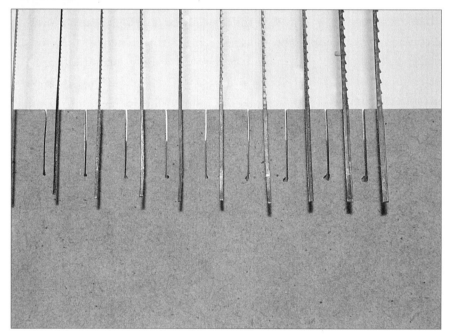

4-12. Ten different-sized blades are shown with their respective spin gaps, the opening generated by rotation of the workpiece. It is clear that the width of the blade, relative to its thickness, determines the difference in size between the kerf and the spin gap.

on-the-spot turns with smaller blades and leave almost no sign of a spin gap because the difference between their width and thickness is very small. This also exemplifies the invalidity of trying to make on-the-spot turns by switching off the machine. While the scroll saw is off, the saw slot will grip the blade. Since the blade width is greater than its thickness, it is not possible to turn the workpiece without twisting the blade in the process. This would likely ruin the blade, maybe even break it, when the machine is restarted. Refer to 6-10 in Cutting Circles for information on how to use on-the-spot turns to cut complete circles.

5 Sawing Wood and Non-Wood Material

A small survey has shown that most scroll-sawyers use the scroll saw to cut wood and wood-based materials. Relatively few used the machine for materials other than wood, yet those who did seemed to have extended their range of materials considerably (5-1).

The chart shown on page 106 lists the range of different materials that can be cut with a scroll saw. I have sawn all of these materials successfully, in some cases after considerable experimentation with regard to blade type, stroke speed, and rate of feed. All of these factors are detailed in Blades, Stroke Speed, and Feed Rate on pages 97 and 98. That section deals exclusively with the cutting of wood-based material, but reference should be made to the information in the section Cutting Wood in this chapter. Also refer to the sections in this chapter that describe how to cut various types of non-wood material. Before making any cuts described in this chapter, refer to Chapter 8, which discusses safety techniques.

Cutting Wood

In choosing a suitable wood, several considerations are pertinent with regard to its nature and its characteristics as a workable material. Features such as color, texture, and grain pattern all combine to produce unique effects.

5-1 (left). All of the materials shown here were cut with a scroll saw. Shown are several types of wood of various thickness, composite board, particleboard, plywood, veneer, textiles, plastics, metals, rubber, linoleum, and cork.

TABLE 5-1

MATERIALS THAT CAN BE CUT WITH A SCROLL SAW

Woods/Wood-Based Material	Metals	Plastics	Miscellaneous
Blockboard	Aluminum	Acrylic	Bone
Density Fiberboard	Brass	Glass-Reinforced Plastic	Carpet Medium-
Particleboard (Faced and Plain)	Copper	Most Dense Plastics	Fiber-Matting
Plywood/Laminated Boards	Steel	Polyvinylchloride	Ceramics
Solid Wood (Hard and Softwood)		Soft Plastic Foam	Cork
Veneers			Glass
			Ivory
			Leather
			Linoleum
			Rubber

Many softwoods have a pronounced grain, consisting of narrow, darker growth that occurs in the winter interspersed with wider, paler growth that occurs in the summer. Depending on the tree's rate of growth, the grain will be either wide or narrow. Fast-growing species have a wider grain. The difference in hardness between hard and soft grain can be startling, leading to the need for caution when sawing.

Hardwoods are more dense that softwoods, so they have a closer grain, but there are prime examples of spectacular wild-grain patterns that can produce unexpected variations in texture (5-2 and 5-3).

Whether cutting softwood or hardwood, be cautious when applying forward pressure at the blade. Be alert to changes in density and grain irregularities that may affect blade performance. Ideally, there would be a different blade pattern to suit each type of operation. However, the

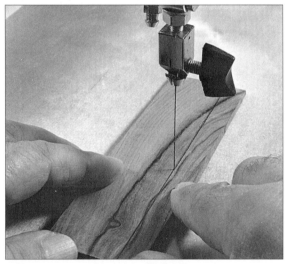

5-2. When cutting wavy, wild grain, it is necessary to be alert to the changes in grain that tend to deflect the blade during sawing.

5-3 (right). The grain, whether it is wavy or straight, will influence blade bias if the blade is following circular or curved saw lines.

disposition of the scroll saw is such that it can be used to cut in all directions within the same workpiece. A blade with a good design will accommodate all these differences, but operator awareness is necessary to achieve the best results.

In general, particleboard and medium-density fiberboard may be treated similarly to solid hardwood, except that the normal considerations of grain content do not apply. Most man-made boards contain more hard resins and adhesives so they are consequently harder on the blade, requiring more frequent blade changes. As with other sawing, manual or with machines, a cleaner sawn edge is obtainable from medium-density fiberboard than particleboard.

Cutting Metal

Metals vary in density and hardness to an enormous degree. Also, their resistance to sawing varies, and not necessarily in proportion to their hardness. There are also great differences in the properties of different types of the same metal, for example between mild steel and high-speed steel and hard brass and soft brass. Compare high-density metal such as lead to a low-density one such as brass, to find that the brass is about 20 times as hard as the lead. Ferrous metals, irons, and steels vary very little in their densities, but tremendously in hardness. For example, high-speed steel is about 60 percent harder than mild steel.

Despite the enormous range in density and hardness that can be found among metals, most common metals can be sawn under the correct conditions. Follow these guidelines:

1. Use a metal-cutting blade (5-4). These blades have little or no set and do not have a skip-tooth design. Use a finer blade, slower stroke speed, and a gentle rate of feed.

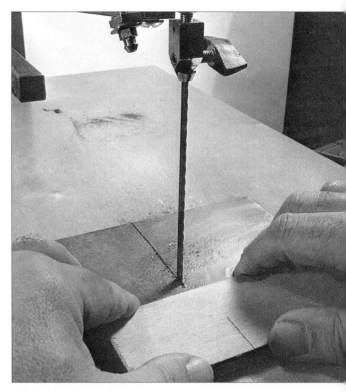

5-4. *This metal-cutting hacksaw blade is cutting a brass sheet. To assist in hand control, attach a wooden pad to the top of the sheet with double-sided adhesive tape.*

2. Apply a liquid coolant to the cutting area to help dissipate the heat and lubricate the cutting action (5-5). This reduces friction between the blade and the workpiece. The coolant can be applied by brush directly to the blade, but this requires the temporary removal of the operator's hand from the workpiece. A better alternative is to apply the liquid via an independent control. For this, a coolant reservoir works well. Hegner has a scroll saw that incorporates a foot pump that supplies the coolant without the need to stop the machine.

3. For the sawing of parts requiring great precision it is recommended to use a hold-down and blade support or, better yet, an accessory such as the Diamond Tool-Bridge.

5-5. *Cutting steel with a thin blade with fine teeth at a moderate speed. The nozzle is adjusted to provide cooling air that, in this case, is a constant stream produced by an independent pump, not by a bellows blowing intermittently.*

4. Lengthy sessions of metalwork can be tiring to the fingers and eyes, so use a foot switch. A foot switch allows rest stops during the progress.

5. The edge left on the workpiece after it has been sawn can be as sharp as a knife blade, so handle it with respect until it has been dulled with emery paper or some other metal abrasive. This is an additional reminder that it is always prudent to wear safety glasses for eye protection during sawing operations, particularly when cutting materials.

Refer to Accessory for Cutting Thin Wood or Metal and Coolant Dispenser on pages 49 to 51 for more information on accessories that aid in cutting metal.

Cutting Plastics

Plastics can be grouped into two types: hard and soft, or rigid and flexible. A very rigid plastic is likely to be of dense material and relatively hard.

Follow these guidelines when cutting hard or soft plastics:

1. When cutting hard plastic, use a coarse blade without too wide a set and with a skip-tooth pattern at a slow stroke speed and with a moderate feed rate. If too fast a speed is used, or if a fine blade is fed at a slow feed rate, it is likely that the material will be burned and that the heat would actually re-weld the pieces together after the blade has passed, leaving just a weld line.

2. Before cutting plastic, attach adhesive tape to the surface above and below the saw line, to help prevent break-out (5-6). Some plastic sheets come with cover sheets that work as an admirable reinforcement (5-7).

5-6. *Adhesive tape is applied to the hard plastic to reduce tear-out on its bottom edge.*

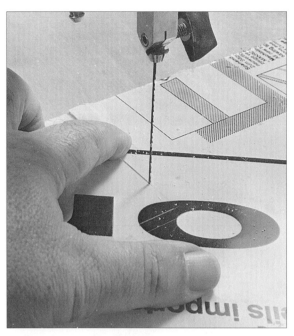

5-7. *The upper face of the plastic sheet is already protected by a cover sheet.*

3. Soft plastics of the non-rigid kind may be cut too, but those that resemble cloth or fabric are best cut with scrap sheets of plywood or medium-density fiberboard. Sandwiching the fabric between the plywood or medium-density fiberboard retains its shape for the sawing process. The cut edge is also acceptable when cut under these conditions, with a fine saw running fairly fast with a moderate feed rate (5-8).

Cutting Ivory, Bone, and Imitations

Ivory and bone can be cut in the same way as hardwood. Imitation ivory and bone should be cut differently, however. This material, if over 1 inch thick, may heat up if it is being cut with

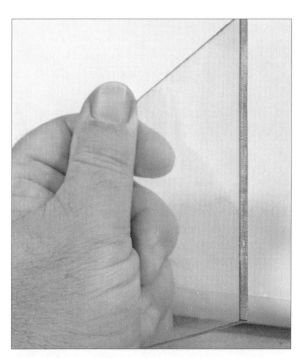

5-8. *Moderation is the key in all respects when cutting plastic, to avoid splintering and burning. Note the excellent saw cut that can be achieved if the proper conditions are met.*

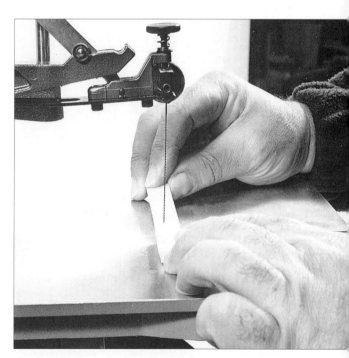

5-9. *Cutting bone is not difficult if it is treated like dense wood, but remember the material can pose a severe health risk if the dust is inhaled.*

too fine a blade and at too high a speed, because the material is a plastic. In this case, treat it as you would plastic, so refer to the Cutting Plastics section that precedes this.

Genuine ivory and bone cut superbly at any thickness using a moderate blade speed and feed rate and a blade that is neither too coarse nor too fine (5-9). If a touch of colorless hard soap is applied to the blade, not only will the operation go smoothly, but the resulting finish on the cut sides will shine.

Cutting Ceramics, Glass, and Stone

Special toothless blades made from round rod coated in abrasive are ideal for cutting ceramics, glass, and stone (5-10). This coating is an extremely hard grit bonded to the steel rod, and is used to literally grind away the hard materials.

When cutting ceramics and glass, it is best to run the blades at fairly slow speeds to reduce burning and also help control the cutting action. There is a tendency for the rod to pick up the workpiece, and this increases the risk of breakage. A coolant works well if any quantity is to be sawn. Even plain water is a help, because the slurry (the mixture of water and material residue) generated by the abrasion will also help dissipate the heat during cutting.

Some natural or synthetic stones can be very hard. I barely scratched one stone after trying to cut it for several minutes, even though I tried to

cut it at both fast and slow speeds, and at high and low feed rates. The material in question, floor tiles, was made of terra-cotta. I think it could have been used to pave military-parade grounds! Refer to Abrasive-Coated Rods on page 76 for more information on using abrasive-coated rods.

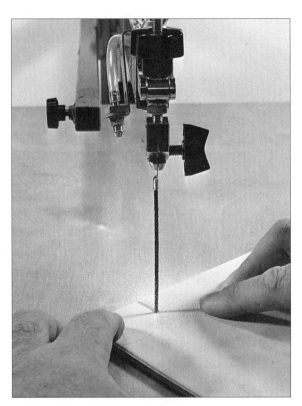

5-10. Ceramic tile being cut with an abrasive rod retained by its cross-pins like a pin-end blade. It is coated with abrasive, so the blade will cut in all directions, obviating the need to rotate the workpiece if curved cutting is required.

6 Cutting Techniques

Crosscutting

Crosscutting is done across the grain of the workpiece (6-1). A crosscut is the most straightforward cut of them all, whether it is made in softwood or hardwood (6-2). Whether the grain pattern is straight or wavy matters little in this operation except on occasions where a specific stop is required in the sawing to satisfy a particular length of cut. The progress of the blade across the growth lines, which alternate from soft to hard, is likely to produce less, rather than more, pressure, respectively. A piece of pine, for example, will make an audible clicking sound as

6-2. *A wide, coarse-toothed blade makes easy work of this 2-inch x 2-inch hardwood block. The blade is a converted band-saw blade and is held by screw-type blade holders. Crosscut applications like this in which the saw cuts across the grain are the least prone to problems associated with grain patterns.*

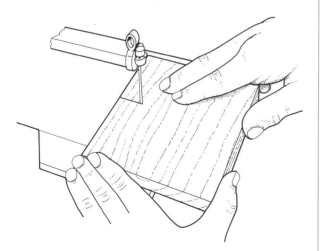

6-1. *A crosscut is a cut made across the grain of the wood.*

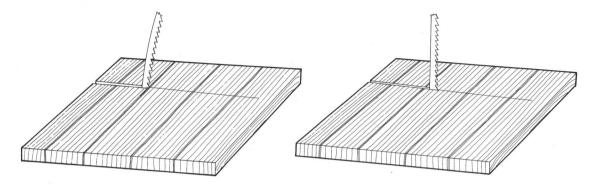

6-3. When sawing across the grain, there is a tendency for the blade to bend under pressure from the resistance of the hard grain, as shown in the drawing on the left. An exaggerated bend in the blade is shown in this illustration. As the blade emerges from the hard grain, meeting less resistance, it tends to spring forward into the soft grain, as shown on the right. In this situation, more care must be given to maintain control of the cutting operation, particularly if the saw path is curved.

the blade cuts the alternating grain densities. If a stop is required on an area with soft grain, extra control of the workpiece is necessary as it leaves the hard grain (6-3). This precaution is essential; otherwise, the blade may spring further than needed into the less-resistant softer area after being deformed by the greater pressure exerted in the area with hard grain.

Rip-Cutting

When straight-line sawing in line with the grain, this is called rip-sawing or rip-cutting (6-4). Referring to the remarks already made about grain structure in the Crosscutting section above, specifically with regard to alternate hard and soft grain, bear the following in mind: Rip-sawing

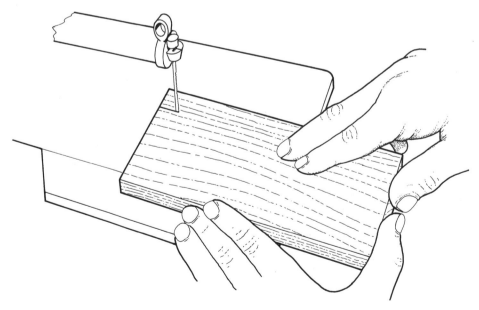

6-4. A rip cut is made with the wood grain.

with the grain means that diagonal crossing of the grain is inevitable, since no wood grows completely straight. A line drawn with a straightedge will possibly cross over from hard to soft grain and maybe back again in a few inches. Each time a deviation is encountered, the blade will try to veer away from the hard grain, seeking an easier route. At these points, in order to overcome this tendency of the blade, the feed rate must be slowed down and extra pressure applied to the side of the workpiece with the hard grain. This must all be done with the lightest touch and total care, because if the pressure is too sudden or too great, the blade will overcome the resistance of the hard grain too abruptly and plunge into the soft area. Some restraint is necessary at the moment the blade exits the hard grain to prevent this tendency to enter too far into the soft grain. The extra pressure on the blade will actually deform its shape as it encounters the hard grain only to be released like a spring on leaving it. A newcomer to the scroll saw attempting a straight-line cut in this situation may well produce something resembling a zigzag pattern instead.

Cutting Curves

Much of the information in Crosscutting and Rip Cut applies here (6-5). Remember, up to a point the harder the wood, the easier it is to control the blade, since generally it has a more uniform texture. But beware of exceptions. Just when I think I have learned about a particular species of wood, I come across some renegade specimen that seems to be willfully nonconformist!

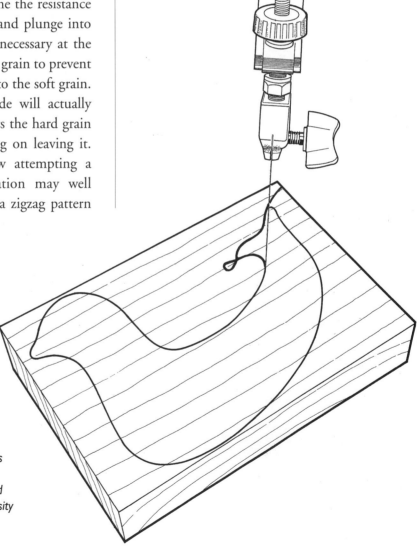

6-5. *A series of curves is being followed here, including a loop to negotiate a sharp point. As the alternating hard and soft grains are met, the sawyer must adjust the pressure on the blade to control it and prevent it from "springing" as the density of the wood varies.*

Cutting Circles

Most often, circles will be needed for parts such as wheels that are complete in themselves and not attached to another part. In these cases, the blade's entry hole should be as inconspicuous as possible to ensure smooth operation. Two methods are recommended for experimentation. Either will work, so the choice is left to the individual. Method One consists of approaching the scribed circle at an angle and gradually aligning the path of the blade with that of the circumfer-

CUTTING CIRCLES

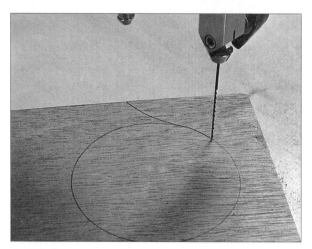

6-6. There are two methods of cutting complete circles. In the first one, shown here, the blade enters the circle at a slight angle.

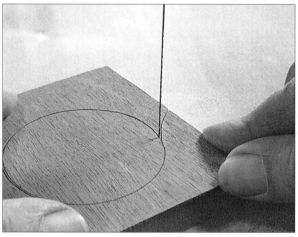

6-7. As the circle is completed and the kerf meets up with itself, make sure the side of the blade does not slip into the entry slot.

6-8. Despite great care, it is still possible to leave a bump on the side of the workpiece at the intersection of the kerf. This bump can be removed with the blade or with a sanding block.

6-9. If a bulge occurs as a result of joining two ends of a sawline, it may be removed easily with an abrasive block.

CUTTING CIRCLES (CONTINUED)

6-10. *In the second method of cutting complete circles, the blade approaches the circle straight on, and then the operator performs a 90-degree on-the-spot turn to cut the entire circle. This technique is probably superior to the one shown in 6-6 and 6-7. It leaves an almost blemish-free circle.*

ence of the circle (6-6 and 6-7). The blade follows the peripheral saw line until it reaches the entry point. The point of entry will be virtually invisible.

Remember, there is an inevitable tendency for the blade to kick away from the circle into the entry slot just before the entry point is reached. The result is a tiny bulge that protrudes from the otherwise smooth circumference (6-8). Rather than try to smooth this away with the blade, it is probably better to rub it away with an abrasive block (6-9).

The second method involves a different approach and is a potentially superior technique. Plunge the blade straight into the workpiece, striking the circumference of the circle at a radial point. Then swivel the workpiece as would be done when making on-the-spot turns, but only at a 90-degree angle. This aligns the blade with the peripheral line. The blade follows the line around until the entry point is reached. Place the blade precisely into the kerf left at the point of entry. If this technique is executed correctly, virtually no sign of the join will be noticeable (6-10).

Refer to Circle-Cutting Jig on pages 61 to 63 for more information on cutting circles.

Cutting Large Workpieces

Pieces that are longer than the throat depth of the scroll saw can be sawn in two ways. If the machine has swiveling blade holders, simply re-orient the blades to position their teeth to the side rather than in front of the operator (6-11). Long workpieces can then be fed to the blade from the side (6-12).

If no means of swiveling the holder is available, and it is not possible to attach a blade stirrup at right angles to normal, then twisting the blade ends could be the solution. Two pairs of pliers are ideal tools for this job. Hold one end of the blade with one pair of pliers, and grip the part of the blade close to the first pair of pliers with a second pair. Despite the apparent hardness of the blade, it is malleable enough to permit the ends to be twisted 90 degrees (6-13). Now, return the blade to the blade holders and fit it as usual, but with its teeth facing to one side.

Refer to Cutting Workpieces Longer Than The Throat Depth on pages 77 and 78 for additional information on cutting large workpieces.

CUTTING LARGE WORKPIECES

6-11. Some blade holders have additional slots that permit pin-end blades to be installed so that their teeth face to the side of the operator rather than to the front, which allows the cutting of longer workpieces.

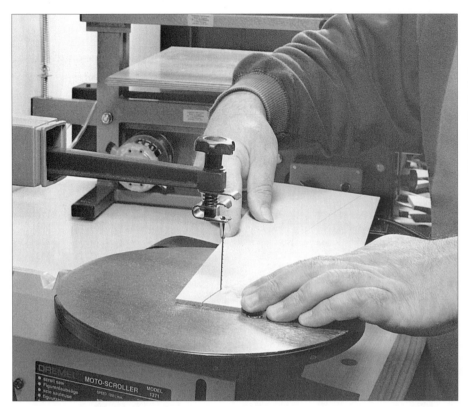

6-12. Workpieces of unlimited lengths can be cut when blade teeth face the side, but heavy pieces being cut on a smaller worktable can pose problems.

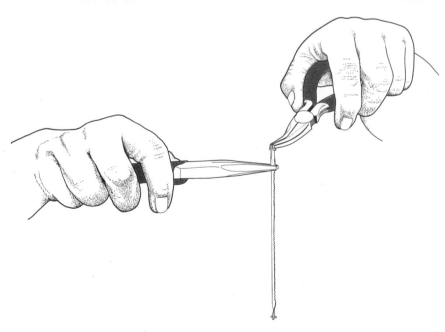

6-13. Two pairs of pliers are used to twist the ends of a pin-end blade. This is to enable the blade to be installed in the holder with its saw teeth facing the side, rather than facing the front of the scroll saw.

Cutting Small Workpieces

Cutting any workpiece around the size of a postage stamp can lead to problems, not merely because it is difficult to manipulate the workpiece but also because it is difficult to support it. Often, the blade hole in the worktable is too large to permit small workpieces to be supported fully, leading to potential hazards. Several solutions are at hand.

If a few square inches of scrap board are available, place the scrap board on the worktable and saw into it, leaving the blade running in the slot. This piece of scrap is, in effect, an ancillary table on which the small workpiece may be placed and cut, since it will be supported completely during the process (6-14 and 6-15). An added advantage is that with such support there will be less likelihood of

CUTTING SMALL WORKPIECES

6-14. Shown here is a fast solution to the problem of cutting a small piece on a worktable with a large blade slot. If no ancillary table is available, simply advance the blade a short distance into a piece of scrap plywood.

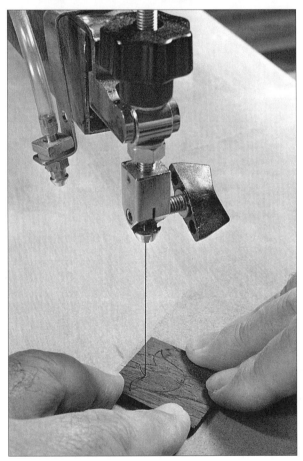

6-15. The workpiece is placed on top of the plywood scrap which serves as an ancillary table. The plywood scrap has an exceptionally well-fitting blade slot.

leaving tear-out on the bottom edge of the cut (6-16).

Another approach is to saw the tiny part from the larger piece, but do not completely sever them. Leave a tiny bit of material that connects the small part to the main stock. This connecting material will be sawn through after the detail work is completed.

Another, better method is to attach the workpiece temporarily to a piece of waste material long enough to move the piece away from the blade. Then saw the workpiece and the waste, and separate the parts. Double-sided adhesive tape is perfect for this, since its adhesion is sufficient to hold the parts together for the sawing process, but is removable (6-17).

It is worth mentioning a trick I saw used by an old sawyer, who put thimbles on his forefingers to allow close, but safe, contact with the saw blade (6-18).

CUTTING SMALL WORKPIECES (CONTINUED)

 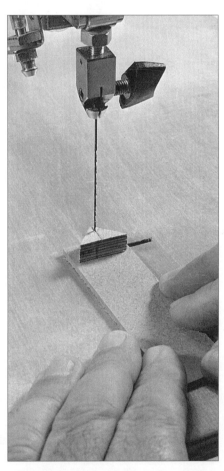 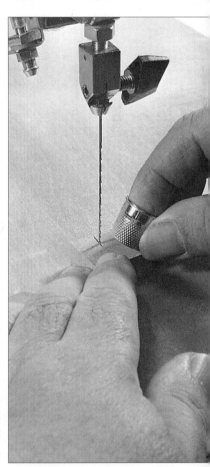

6-16 (left). *An added advantage to the fact that the blade fits closely in the ancillary table is the lack of tear-out on the bottom edge of the workpiece.* **6-17 (center).** *Another way of cutting small pieces safely and securely is to fix the piece to scrap temporarily with adhesive tape and cut both pieces simultaneously.* **6-18 (right).** *Fingers that are too close to the scroll-saw blade can be protected by thimbles. Bear in mind, however, that scroll-saw blades can cut metal!*

Making Templates for Curved Shapes

Templates, made from thin, durable materials cut to the exact size and shape of the desired part, can be used as patterns for decorative scroll-work. Some templates are intricate and delicate, making demands on the steering skills of the sawyer. Rarely does a decorative project require the absolute precision demanded in engineering, of course, but it is good to practice accuracy as a matter of principle.

One of the important keys to making a successful cutout is to plan the saw path, taking into consideration tight bends and sharp corners (6-19 and 6-20). To make a sharp turn, it is

USING TEMPLATES

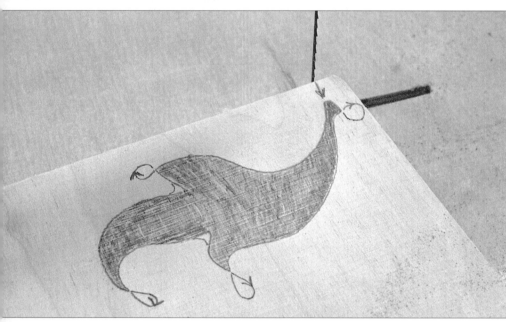

6-19. *Templates intended for stenciling make ideal scroll-sawing patterns. Use a sharp knife to cut the patterns out of the transparent plastic. Note the arrowheads that were added to the pattern to show the sawing route before the pattern is cut.*

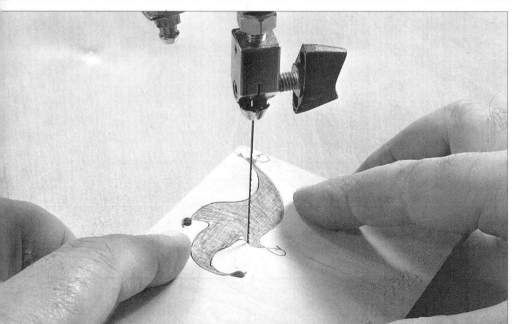

6-20. *After tracing the pattern onto the workpiece, plan a sawing route. To make turns when cutting sharp pointed features, it is often easier to make a loop and then re-enter the saw path.*

often easier to make a loop and re-enter the saw path. In cases where a sharp inside corner occurs, it will be easier for the blade to come out of the bend early, leaving the sharp angle to be cleaned up on a subsequent sawing (6-21 and 6 -22). It may be helpful for a beginner to draw on the extraneous saw lines to indicate the blade's path and to add tracking arrows as a directional guide.

If necessary, templates can be made from printed patterns. One way is to trace around the printed pattern on sturdy drafting paper, cut out the outline, and use the template (6-23 to 6-28).

Another method of cutting patterns is to trace the motif onto semitransparent paper and stick the paper onto the workpiece.

USING TEMPLATES (CONTINUED)

6-21. *Clean up sharp internal corners after the main outline is sawn.*

6-22. *The finished piece cut from ⁵/₁₆-inch-thick birch-faced plywood.*

USING TEMPLATES (CONTINUED)

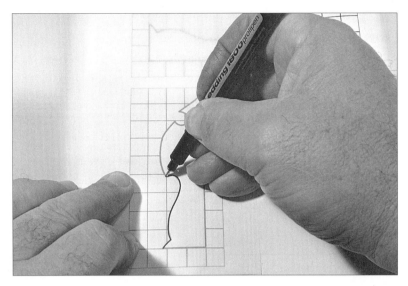

6-23. *One easy way to make a template is to trace around the printed pattern on sturdy drafting film.*

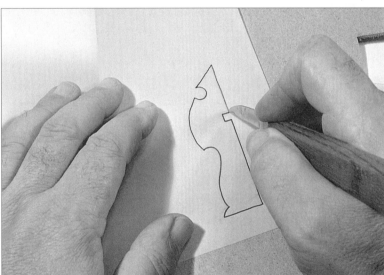

6-24. *After tracing the outline of the pattern, cut it out with a sharp knife.*

6-25. *The cutout can be used either as an internal or external template.*

USING TEMPLATES (CONTINUED)

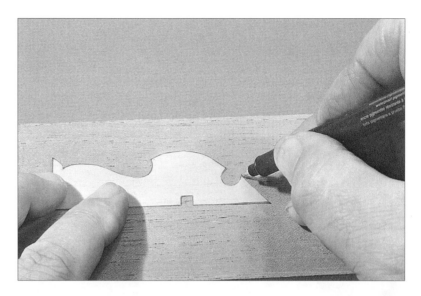

6-26. *Drafting film is stiff enough to perform well as a template.*

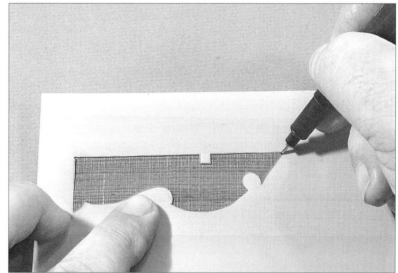

6-27. *Tracing from an internal pattern is more secure traced because it has less of a tendency to buckle.*

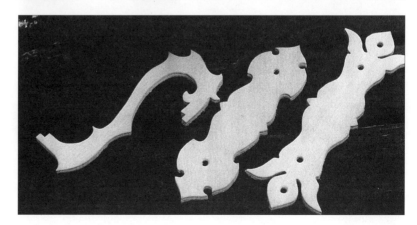

6-28. *All of the pieces shown were made by the template method shown in 6-23 to 6-27 with a basic single-speed scroll saw with a fine, pin-end blade.*

Internal-Sawing

Internal-sawing, or pierced-work, consists of cutting apertures. It is no different from external sawing except that it requires insertion of the blade through an access hole in the workpiece. Some discretion is necessary as to where to locate the access hole, for practical and artistic reasons. Let's take as an example a design that merely requires the outline of a pattern with simple entry-hole shapes to be cut. In such a case, line intersections are good places to put the access holes. They will work well in the corners of a pattern, where a hole can help the blade navigate a sharp turn. If the hole is curved, remember to refer to the two ways of cutting out a circle described in Cutting Circles on pages 114 and 115. Try both ways. Before embarking on the sawing, determine whether to begin by cutting the holes or the exterior outline first (6-29 to 6-32). It will probably be better to cut the holes first, particularly if the finished design is delicate.

INTERNAL-SAWING

6-29. *Another method of cutting patterns is to trace the motif onto semitransparent paper and stick the paper onto the workpiece. Prepare for internal-sawing or piercing work by considering the most practical points of blade entry. Sharp inside corners make good starting points.*

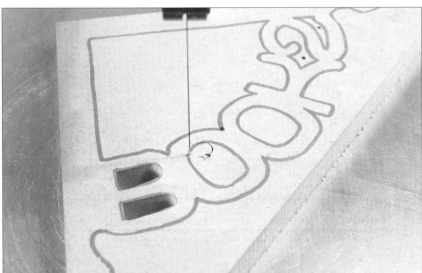

6-30. *When cutting inside openings, either start on the line or enter the opening from somewhere in the waste from a spiral.*

INTERNAL-SAWING (CONTINUED)

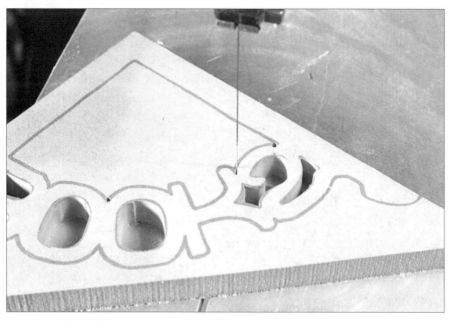

6-31. *Internal-sawing cuts such as the one shown here give several opportunities to practice on-the-spot turns.*

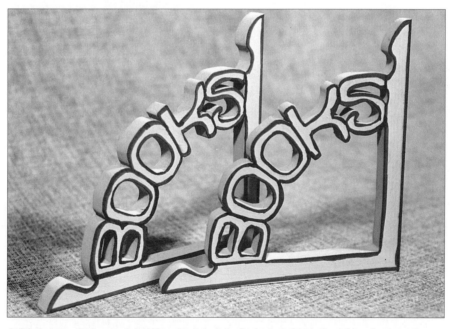

6-32. *A pair of identical designs, the second of which was produced by drawing the outline of the first one onto the workpiece. If the material were thin enough, both could be cut simultaneously.*

Marquetry

BOULLE METHOD OF STACK-CUTTING VENEER

Marquetry is the technique of cutting and joining different-colored veneers together to create a design that can be glued to another flat surface. André-Charles Boulle, an 18th-century French marquetarian, invented the technique of utilizing stack-sawing techniques (6-33) normally used by scroll sawyers to inlay marquetry, in which several layers of material are cut at a time. This technique, known as Boulle-work, is ideal for the modern craftsman with a scroll saw.

To use the Boulle method of cutting veneer, do the following: Lay different-colored veneers or thin sheets in a stack, at the bottom of which should be waste sheet. Join them together temporarily by gluing them with adhesive, or by pinning or taping together their edges. Draw a design on the upper layer and cut the whole stack simultaneously (6-34 to 6-36).

After separating the layers and discarding the waste sheet, it becomes possible to mix cutouts from one layer with another in order to create contrasting effects (6-37). There is, of course, a gap that separates the top pieces from the bottom ones. This gap was created by the saw kerf. Fill the kerf gaps with a paste made from sawdust and glue (6-38). This is usually applied during the gluing process when the veneer is fixed to whatever surface is to be decorated. After the adhesive has dried, clean and smooth the whole panel to prepare it for a suitable surface finish.

BOULLE MARQUETRY

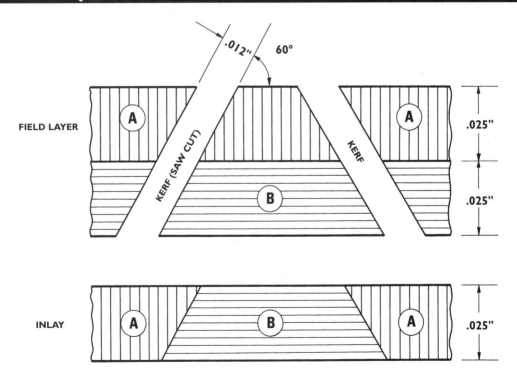

6-33. *Simultaneous cutting of two layers. Cutting two or more layers at a time is called stack-cutting. The intention is to fit the lower inlay (B) to the upper inlay (A) via the saw cuts.*

6-34. In Boulle-work marquetry, several layers of veneer are stacked together and cut. There should be a waste sheet on the bottom of the stack. The veneers are selected for contrast in grain, color, and texture.

6-35. After taping together the layers of veneer with the waste sheet on the bottom, pierce a hole somewhere on the saw line.

6-36. Saw all four layers simultaneously, following the saw line continuously from the blade-entry hole.

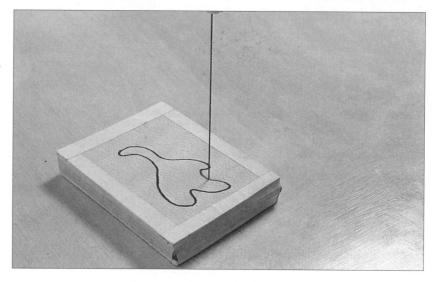

6-37. When the sawing is completed, separate all four layers and discard the waste sheet. Mix the cutouts and the surrounding material to create contrasting effects.

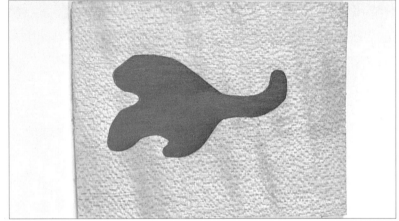

6-38. The kerf gaps are filled with a paste made of sawdust and glue.

"FLAWLESS" MARQUETRY

In "flawless" marquetry, the motifs are inlaid without discernible gaps or space between them and the backing material (6-39). Layers of wood are stack-cut as described in Hollow-Form Intarsia on pages 134 to 136. Prepare these layers as described in that section with the exception that three layers are used instead of four, with one of these layers a bottom waste piece (6-40). It is important that the table is correctly angled so that the pattern fits perfectly into the cutout section (6-41). Some trial and error may be necessary to determine the required tilt, depending on the thickness of the layers and the width of the blade.

After sawing the layers, separate them, dispose of the waste material, and fit the top cutout into the opening cut out of the second layer (6-42 and 6-43). If the sawing angle, blade thickness, and material thickness are coordinated correctly, a flawless inlay should appear, with no gaps between the joined parts.

"FLAWLESS" MARQUETRY

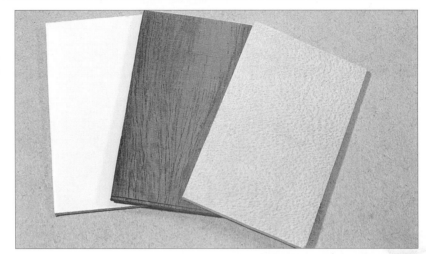

6-39. *"Flawless" marquetry is produced by creating an insert exactly the same size as the cut-out area into which it will be placed. This is a matter of coordinating the thickness of material, sawing angle, and blade thickness. Shown here are the layers of wood that will be stack-cut.*

6-40. *Stack the layers together, with the material intended for the surround on top. Trace the outline of the motif ready for sawing and pierce a blade-entry hole into the top layer at the required angle.*

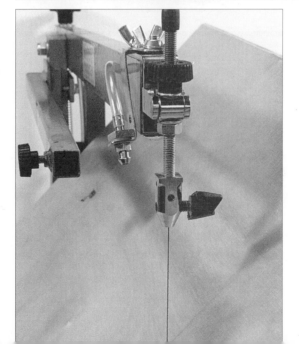

6-41. *The table angle is determined by calculations or by experimentation, if prefered.*

6-42. All three layers have been cut simultaneously and separated.

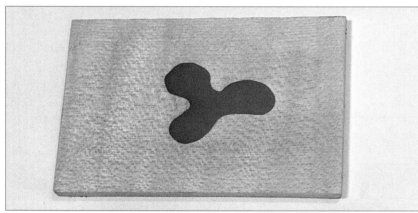

6-43. The motif cut from the lower layer fits into the opening cut out of the upper layer. The taper on the edges of the motif ensures a good fit and verifies that the correct table-angle calculations were used.

Intarsia

INTARSIA WITH WEDGE INLAYS

Intarsia is a technique in which a wood motif is cut out and fitted onto a supporting piece. An effective, yet simple, means of creating intarsia with wedge inlays is possible when the piece is sawn with the worktable set at an angle slightly more than horizontal. The piece is cut from the middle of the panel at an angle of between 5 and 10 degrees (6-44 to 6-49).

After the sawing is completed, the piece is placed back in the area from which it was cut. Because the kerf caused by the blade has removed some material from the panel, the inlay is wedged into the panel and extends from it. It appears almost as if the inlay were carved from the panel, since both the panel and the inlay have the same grain features (6-50 and 6-51).

INTARSIA WITH WEDGE INLAYS

6-44. *A wedge inlay is a simple but effective way to produce a decorative panel. Any method of marking the motif on the panel will do. A paper pattern is being used in this example.*

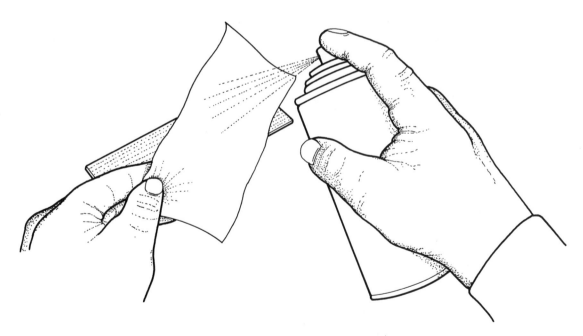

6-45. *A spray-on adhesive of the type used for arranging photographs is deal for fixing the paper pattern to the workpiece because it is possible to position the pattern before fixing it to the workpiece.*

INTARSIA WITH WEDGE INLAYS (CONTINUED)

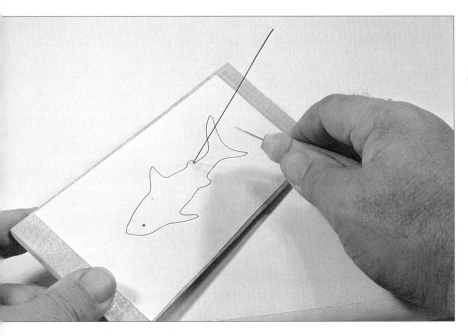

6-46. *Pierce a blade-entry hole in an obtrusive place on the saw line.*

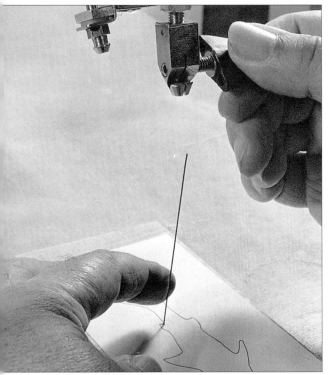

6-47. *Thread the plain-end blade into the work-piece before attaching it to the blade holders.*

6-48. *For this type of inlay, the table is inclined between 6 and 10 degrees. The greater the inclination, the less the motif will protrude from the surround.*

INTARSIA WITH WEDGE INLAYS (CONTINUED)

6-49. Cut the outline, always keeping the saw on the marked line and maintaining a consistent angle.

6-50. This cutout was sawn at an angle at about 8 degrees. The saw kerf is about .020 inch wide, and the wood cut is around $3/16$ inch thick. This allows almost the whole depth of the motif to protrude from the opening it is fitted in. The motif was wiped with coffee and a coat of Danish oil, which contrasts it nicely with the surround. The grain patterns common to both parts make the fish appear as if under water.

6-51. This view shows how little of the motif is hidden by the surround or supporting material. Just a dab of glue was enough to fix it to the surround.

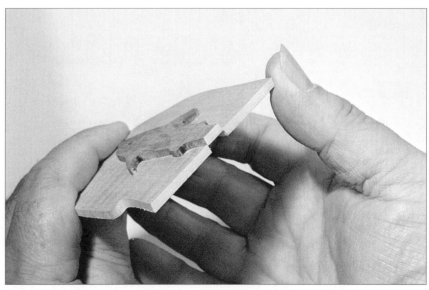

HOLLOW-FORM INTARSIA

Hollow-form intarsia is created in the same way as intarsia with wedge inlays except that instead of a single layer, four layers are stacked and cut together (6-52). The order of layers from the top is: wood veneer that contains the pattern, waste layer, wood veneer, waste layer (6-53 and 6-54). The two veneer layers should be of contrasting woods, while the waste can be of cardboard. The waste layer between the two veneers creates a gap that provides a difference in the size of the two veneers. The waste layer at the bottom prevents the lower veneer from splintering.

HOLLOW-FORM INTARSIA

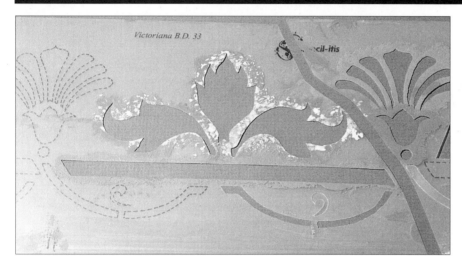

6-52. Hollow-form intarsia is a new method of creating decorative inlays. In this example, a simple leaf shape is used as a pattern.

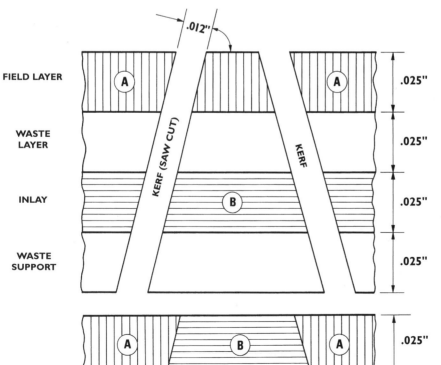

6-53. In hollow-form intarsia, four layers are stacked and cut together. Shown is the arrangement of a typical four-layer stack.

Join the layers together by taping them around their edges (6-55). Do not glue them or pin their edges. This is excessive. Then draw a motif or pattern on the top layer (6-56 and 6-57), and cut it out about 15 degrees off the horizontal (6-58). After cutting out the motif, remove it from the workpiece (6-59) and separate the workpiece into individual layers. Discard the waste pieces

and insert the top layer into the area from which the third layer was cut out. The effect is of a cleverly sawn intarsia, framed in a surround with a delicate parallel gap between the intarsia and the surround. Mounted on a contrasting background, the intarsia has an attractive appearance (6-60).

HOLLOW-FORM INTARSIA (CONTINUED)

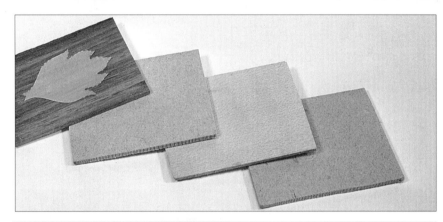

6-54. Four layers are stacked together and cut. The top and third layers are wood. The second and bottom layers are waste material.

6-55. All four layers are stacked and taped together with adhesive tape in the order described in 6-54.

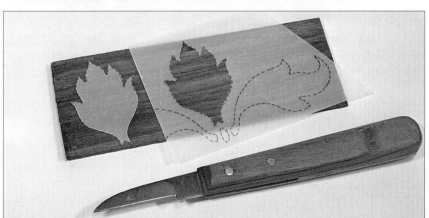

6-56. A knife was used to cut the template out of drafting paper.

HOLLOW-FORM INTARSIA (CONTINUED)

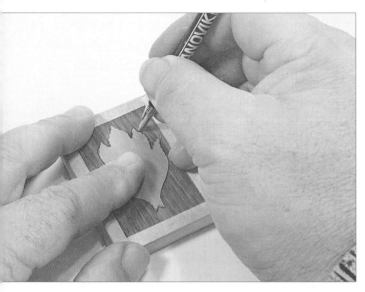

6-57. Trace the pattern on the top layer that will eventually become the inlay.

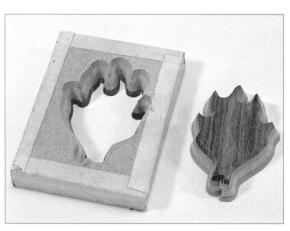

6-59. After completing the sawing operation, disassemble the pieces and discard everything but the motif for the top layer and the surround from the third layer.

6-58. Drill the blade-entry hole at about 65 degrees to the horizontal. Then saw the outline at the same table setting.

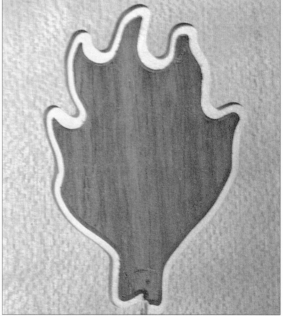

6-60. Glue both selected parts on to a white backing panel, with the motif arranged in the middle of the panel to leave an equal gap all around the panel. Parts of different thickness may be used to give contrasting effects between the two parts.

Sawing with a Spiral Blade

Sawing with a spiral blade is somewhat different from using a standard blade because there is a cutting edge all around the blade, so the workpiece can be maneuvered to approach the blade from any direction. If the worktable is set at an angle, an interesting effect is achieved by keeping the workpiece oriented in one direction while cutting a design with the blade. A good example is that of cutting letters that form a name or any other words. These can be made with a spiral blade and letter guides (6-61 to 6-63).

6-61. *Letter guides are a rapid and entertaining way to create customized messages. The ones shown here are made of plastic. The set includes upper- and lower-case letters and numbers.*

6-62. *Creating letters with the guide is straightforward. A pencil or felt-tipped pen is used to inscribe the outlines.*

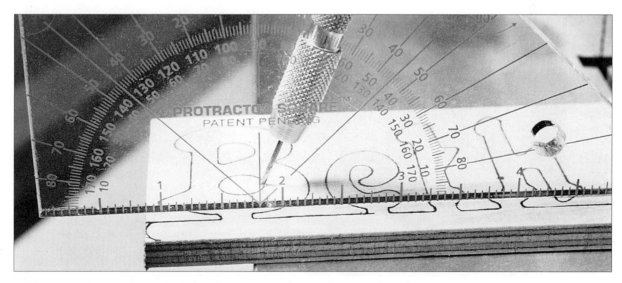

6-63. *Some of the letters have apertures, of course, so, therefore, a blade entry hole must be created. In this case, the holes are pierced at an angle to suit the sawing angle. The intention is to cut the letters at an angle of about 20 degrees, to enhance the perspective.*

Begin by tilting the table and approaching the blade with the front edge of the workpiece parallel to the front edge of the worktable (6-64 and 6-65). This must be maintained as the outline of the letters is cut by the blade. The lower edges on the letters may have to be cleaned up (6-66).

Fixed to a panel of contrasting material, the nameplate has an interesting effect in that it seems to be leaning (6-67 to 6-69).

Refer to Spiral Blades on pages 75 and 76 for more information on spiral blades.

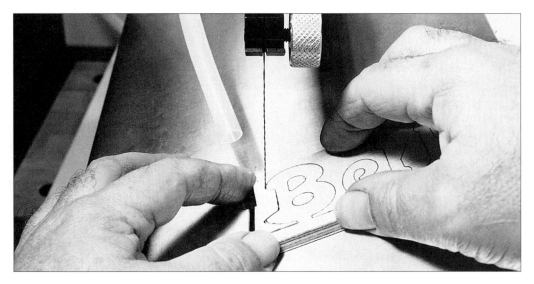

6-64. *Sawing may begin after setting the table at the corresponding angle to suit the pierced holes. A spiral drill is necessary to produce the beveled effect because the workpiece must be kept at the same orientation while the blade navigates the outlines.*

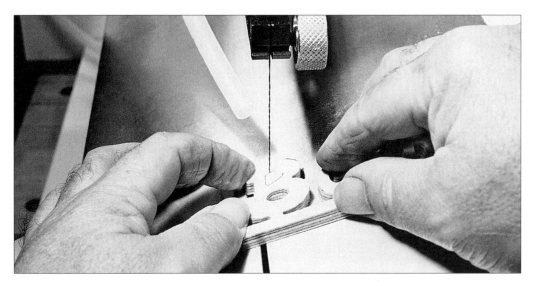

6-65. *Quick-change blade holders are sensible for this type of work where many openings are included in the pattern.*

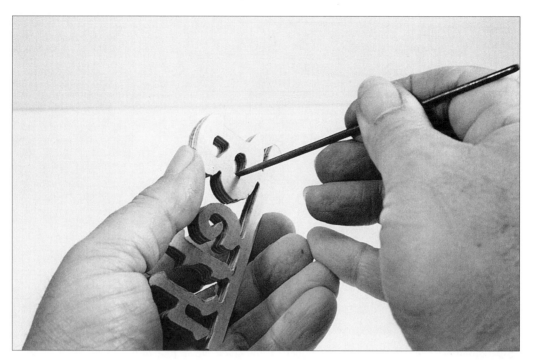

6-66. *It is necessary to clean up the lower edges to remove some ragged corners left by the relatively coarse spiral blade.*

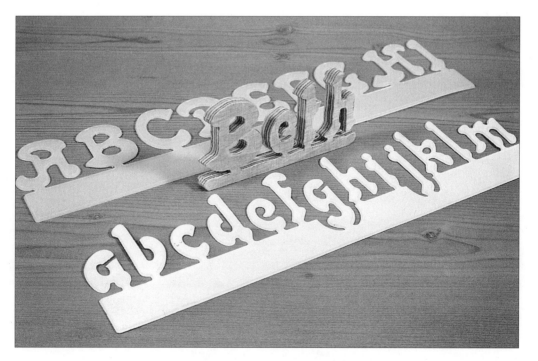

6-67. *Plywood works well for this type of project, because it is, if compared to wood of equal size, much sturdier.*

6-68. A cabinet scraper is being used to flatten and clean the surface of a backing panel of dark hardwood to prepare it for a finish. With a few coats of oil, the panel is darkened to make a handsome contrast with the name.

6-69. The finished nameplate.

CHAPTER **7** **Patterns**

Patterns are an important part of scroll-saw work, being used to provide the designs for projects. The pattern is transferred to the wood and then cut out. There are many sources for patterns, including woodworking books, magazines, and commercial patterns sold through catalogue houses and mail-order companies.

Copying and Transferring Patterns

Patterns are usually found in magazines or woodworking books. In most cases they are printed smaller than full size and, therefore, need to be increased to a size suitable for the needs of the individual. If the pattern is printed with an overlaid grid of squares, so much the better, because this enables the production of an enlarged pattern to be made easily for transfer to the workpiece. If the chosen design does not have a grid of squares, it is easy to draw on the lines with a rule. Decide on whether the pattern is to be the same size or enlarged and choose a workpiece big enough to accommodate it. If it is preferred to produce a pattern on paper to tranfer to the workpiece, then a piece of paper should be prepared.

Assuming the pattern is to be enlarged to three times the size of the original and drawn on a piece of paper for transfer to the work-piece, proceed as follows. If the grid on the original design is made of ¼-inch squares, then the grid to be drawn on the enlarged pattern must be of ¾-inch squares. This will produce a copy of the original enlarged three times. Count the ¼-inch squares on the pattern and draw as many ¾-inch squares on the paper prepared for the enlarged copy. Mark a small dot wherever the outline of the design intersects a grid-line on both the design and the copy. Do this square by square until the whole design is translated as a series of dots on the paper. It is then a simple matter to join up the dots, referring to the original from time to time to maintain accuracy (7-1). This will produce an enlarged pattern ready to stick down on a workpiece ready for scroll-sawing.

Another way to copy and enlarge or reduce a pattern is to use a pantograph (7-2). A pantograph has three main elements: a base, a tracing-point, and a pencil-end. Hold the base of the pantograph firmly on a work surface, with the tracing-point over the design to be copied and the pencil on the paper ready to draw the copy. As the tracing-point follows the lines of the design, the pencil reproduces it on the paper. Depending on the positioning of the tracing-point and the pencil on the bars of the pantograph, the copy is either enlarged or reduced.

A fast alternative is to make a copy of a printed

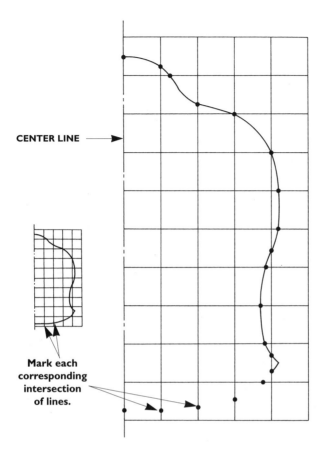

CENTER LINE →

**Mark each
corresponding
intersection
of lines.**

7-1. Enlarging a pattern. First, draw a grid of squares to represent the intended pattern. Then mark dots to show where the outline of the shape intersects with grid lines. Next, connect the marked dots to complete the new pattern.

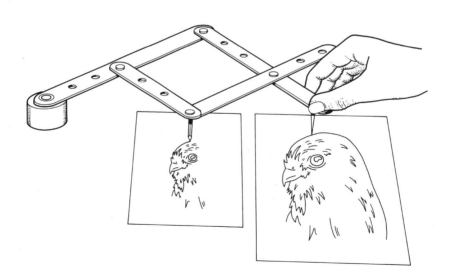

7-2. A pantograph can be used to copy and enlarge or reduce a pattern. The arms of the pantograph can be set to draw the pattern in various scales. In this case, the tracing point follows the pattern outline, and the pencil draws a copy reduced in scale. It is possible to reverse the positions of the tracing point and the pencil to produce copies of a larger size.

design on a photocopying machine that has the facility to enlarge the printed image.

A commercial or user-made pattern may be drawn around with a pencil, to produce a full-size copy directly onto the surface of the workpiece (7-3). An outline may be traced on any design printed on paper by applying a pounce wheel. This is an ancient tool consisting of a wheel with spikes that pierce the paper pattern, leaving a row of tiny holes in the surface of the workpiece (7-4). When drawing the pattern directly, use a compass, straightedge, or other aid to ensure that the layout is geometrically accurate.

Applying the Pattern to the Wood

When sticking the pattern directly to the workpiece, a choice of adhesives is available. One of the rubber-based cements will do. A spray adhesive of the kind used to affix photographs temporarily can also be used. It is better in every case to apply the glue to pattern rather than to the workpiece. It makes sense to follow any special instructions shown by the manufacturer on the label, of course. Rubber-based types allow any surplus adhesive that may be squeezed out from the edge of the pattern to be removed by rubbing with a fingertip.

Using Templates As Patterns

Templates are thin, durable materials cut to the exact size and shape of the desired part. Hardboard, plastic, plywood, and other materials can be used as templates provided they are thin enough, about ⅛ inch thick.

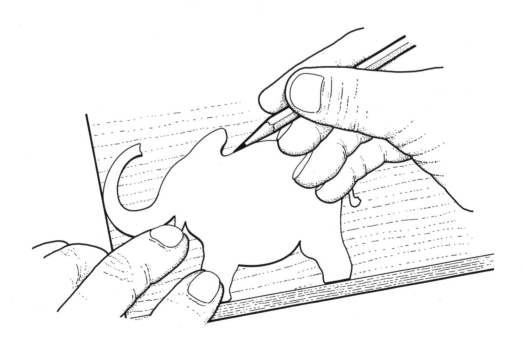

7-3. *Using a commercial or user-made pattern to mark an outline to follow with the blade. It makes sense to draw some of the pattern's extremities on the edge of the workpiece to facilitate the blade-entry hole.*

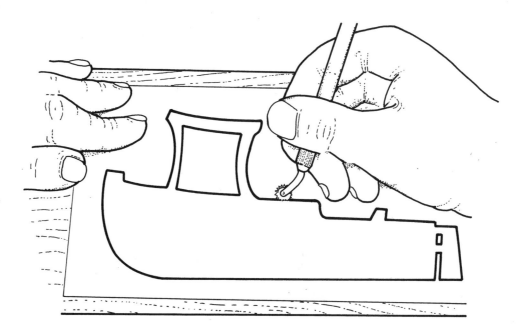

7-4. *Tracing an outline with a pouncing wheel. The sharp points penetrate the pattern, leaving the outline as a row of tiny holes.*

The key to cutting a template is to plan the saw path, including ways to maneuver tight bends and sharp corners. One way to help cut the template successfully is to draw on the saw lines to indicate the blade's path. Beginners should also draw arrows that indicate the correct sawing path. This and other pertinent information is detailed in Making Templates for Curved Shapes on pages 120 to 123.

CHAPTER 8

Safety Procedures

This chapter may be regarded by most wood-workers as boring. It is certainly not inspiring, and discusses nothing that will be of aesthetic value to the woodworker. But above all, it is essential reading for every serious scroll-saw operator, so don't skip it!

Scroll saws are not likely to turn on their gentle owners and savage them without provocation, but hazards may be encountered, particularly when the owner is indifferent to a few safety procedures. To help avoid potential hazards, pay attention to the following instructions, which are not prioritized:

1. Keep the workshop door locked when not in use, to keep out children or the inexperienced.

2. Read the manufacturer's instructions, taking note of any special precautions that are recommended.

3. Double-check wiring, connections, plugs, and sockets in the electric power supply, verifying that they comply with prevailing regulations and are compatible with the machine specifications. The scroll saw should be properly grounded (earthed).

4. During maintenance programs and any other situations that involve a hands-on application, with the exception of the sawing operations, disconnect the machine from the power supply.

5. Make sure the on-off switch on any machinery is switched to "off" before activating the power supply.

6. Clear debris and clutter from the workshop floor, particularly around the machine area.

7. Arrange lighting to the best advantage. This includes the lights in the workshop and the lights on the scroll saw. Refer to pages 47 and 48 for more information on lighting.

8. Isolate and lock away, preferably in a steel cabinet, all flammable materials, such as varnish, paint thinners, cleaners, lubricants, etc.

9. Remember, a piece of used steel wool charged with waste rubbings from varnished work is a dormant explosive predisposed to spontaneous combustion if conditions are favorable!

10. When sawing thick workpieces, try to avoid placing fingers on top of the piece and passing them under the moving arm. Severe pinching of the fingers may ensue, resulting in a release of pressure on the workpiece. This allows the blade to pick up the workpiece and batter it against the table. This may cause damage to the operator's fingers, the table, and the blade.

11. Keep the workpiece thickness within the limits specified by the manufacturer, to reduce hazards and also to minimize wear and tear on the machine.

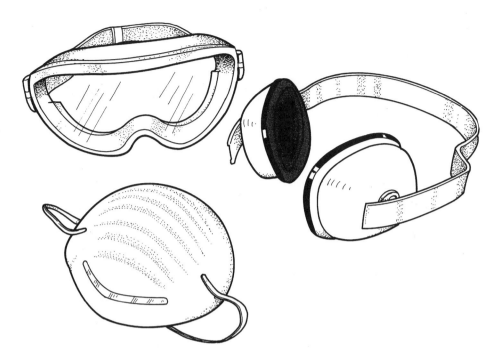

8-1. Workshop protection of various types. Shown are goggles that protect eyes from flying chips, a facemask to filter dust-laden air, and ear protection against prolonged or excessive noise.

12. When sawing, keep fingers away from the front of the moving blade and to the side of the blade.

13. Wear safety glasses if cutting metals or any hard materials that have a tendency to splinter (8-1 and 8-2). Goggles will help to keep dust out of the eyes.

14. Remember, any kind of dust is harmful, so use a regulation dust mask at all times during a sawing session (8-3). The dust doesn't go away when the sawing stops. It is likely to remain for some time after the scroll saw had been switched off, so keep the mask on for a few minutes longer.

15. For any prolonged sessions, use an air filter of the kind that removes dust as small as 1 micron in size (8-4 and 8-5). Dust extractors are rarely equipped to cope with fine dust, and only remove heavier chips and shavings that are not so harmful.

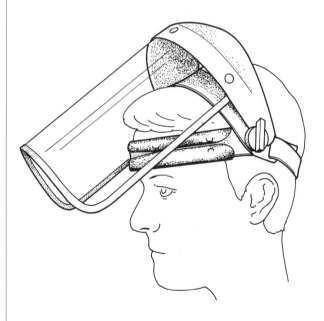

8-2. This full-face visor protects the operator from airborne chips and other flying material.

16. Develop the habit of switching off the scroll saw when each sawing session is finished. Don't leave it running while preparing for the next stage or considering the next project.

17. Observe the advice given in Maintaining Scroll-Saw Components on pages 35 to 38. Set up an individualized program.

18. Make sure the bench or stand is stable and that the machine is fixed securely by bolts or clamps (8-6).

19. Use the guard. As often as not, the more effective the guard, the more it prevents the operator from maneuvering the fingers and the workpiece, so get used to it and become as good a sawyer with the guard as without it.

8-3. *A fabric dust mask that prevents the operator from inhaling dust.*

8-4. *A full face visor that incorporates a battery-driven respirator that delivers filtered air to the user.*

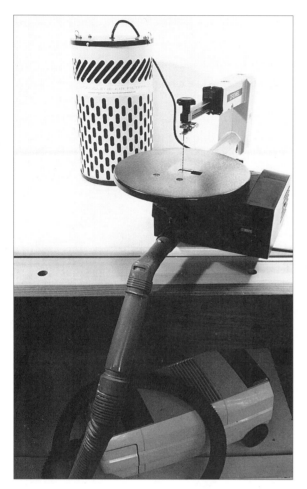

8-5. With the vacuum cleaner extracting sawdust from the sawing area, and the air filter removing fine dust from the atmosphere, most of the harmful wood waste has been collected. To free up work space, the air filter can be suspended over the area.

8-6. Even if the situation is a temporary one and the scroll saw is placed on a non-skid pad, it makes sense to clamp it to the workbench, to minimize the noise and vibration. Bolting is even better, and is desirable if the scroll saw is being used in a permanent location.

20. Considerate machine designers have incorporated a blade-breakage safety device in parallel-arm scroll saws. If the blade breaks, a spring applies tension automatically between the arms at the rear ends. This moves the top arm out of harm's way and stops the movement instantly. The wise operator will discover if his/her machine has such a device and, if so, maintain it regularly. Refer to Blade-Breakage Device on pages 33 and 34 for more information.

Glossary

Ancillary Table A table made from thin material that is used to cover all or part of the original worktable. See Ancillary Table on pages 63 to 65.

Archimede's Drill A drilling device, said to be invented by Archimedes, that is operated by a sliding spool that activates a spiral which, in turn, rotates a drill bit. Archimede's drills are ideal for drilling blade-entry holes. See Awls for Hole-Boring on pages 53 to 55.

Awl (also referred to as a Bodkin) A pointed tool used to pierce blade-entry holes. Awls are usually user-made. See Awls for Hole-Boring on pages 53 to 55.

Blade-Breakage Safety Device A safety device on scroll saws that stops the reciprocating movement of the arms if the blade breaks. See Blade-Breakage Safety Device on pages 33 and 34.

Boulle Marquetry A technique named after an 18th-century French craftsman in which different-colored veneers are stack-sawn and then joined together. See Boulle Method of Stack-Cutting Veneer on pages 126 to 128.

C-Frame Scroll Saw A scroll saw with an open-end frame that resembles an elongated letter C. See C-Frame Scroll Saw on pages 13 to 15.

Crosscut A cut made across the grain of the workpiece. See Crosscutting on pages 111 and 112.

Dust Blower A device that provides a constant flow of air from a motorized pump to clear dust from the sawing area. See Dust Blower on pages 29 and 30.

Dust Puffer A bellows-driven device providing a regular but intermittent supply of air for dust clearance. It relies on the action of the arm for activation.

Dust-Extraction Unit A unit that is fitted to the scroll saw that draws sawdust away from the sawing area. See Dust-Extraction Unit on pages 40 and 41.

Feed Rate Describes the rate at which the material is "fed" to the blade during the sawing operation. See Blades, Stroke Speed, and Feed Rate on pages 97 and 98.

Finger Fence An accessory used to correct a

blade's tendency to cut towards one side. See Finger Fence on pages 59 and 60.

Foot Switch A safety accessory for the scroll saw that allows the operator to turn the saw on and off without use of his hands. See Switches on pages 22 to 25 and Foot Switches on pages 39 and 40.

"Flawless" Marquetry A form of marquetry in which designs are inlaid without any discernible gaps or space between them. See "Flawless" Marquetry on pages 128 to 130.

Flexible Drive or Shaft An accessory attached to and driven by the scroll-saw motor. It has a chuck or collet to hold drill bits and other accessories such as spindle-mounted buffers, abrasives, or cutters. See Flexible Shaft on pages 41 and 42

Guard A safety device used to prevent the fingers of the scroll-sawyer from coming into contact with the blade. See Guards on pages 32 and 33.

Hold-Down A safety device used to keep the material flat on the table and to prevent it from rising up during the sawing operation. See Hold-Down on pages 30 to 32 and 42 to 45.

Hollow-Form Intarsia A type of intarsia that is framed in a surround. The different designs have a parallel gap between them. See Hollow-Form Intarsia on pages 134 to 136.

Intarsia A type of marquetry in which pieces thick enough to permit light relief carving are

used to suggest a three-dimensional effect. See Intarsia on pages 130 to 136.

Internal-Sawing (Also referred to as Pierced Work) Using a scroll saw to cut apertures in a workpiece. See Internal-Sawing on pages 124 and 125.

Kerf The slot or gap made by the saw blade.

"Leaving the Line" Leaving the marked line that defines the area to be sawn for reference-later. See What About the Saw Line? on pages 101 and 102.

Marquetry The technique of cutting and joining different-colored veneers to create a design that can be glued to another flat surface. See Marquetry on pages 126 to 130.

Medium-Density Fiberboard (MDF) A common man-made wood-based panel. Because it is of uniform thickness and lacks directional grain, it has many uses.

NVR Switch A No-Voltage-Release switch that switches to "off" if electrical power is disconnected.

On-the-Spot Turns A technique for sawing sharp inside or outside corners nonstop, requiring the spinning of the workpiece 180 degrees around the blade. See On-the-Spot Turns on pages 102 to 104.

Parallel-Arm Scroll Saw A motorized scroll saw whose upper and lower arms are pivoted independently and interdependently, connected at the rear by a rod and at the front by a saw blade, causing parallel action when reciprocating. See Parallel-Arm Scroll Saw on pages 13 to 21.

Particleboard Sheet material made from wood chips or particles.

Pin-End Blade A scroll-saw blade that has a cross-pin at each end that is retained in a corresponding stirrup arrangement at the ends of the arm of the scroll-saw frame. See Blade Types on pages 73 to 76.

Pitch The distance between the teeth on a blade.

Plain-End Blade A scroll-saw blade that does not have cross-pins. See Blade Types on pages 73 to 76.

Reverse-Tooth Blade A blade with half-a-dozen teeth at the lower end that point upwards, rather than downwards. Reverse-tooth blades do not leave as much tear-out as other types of scroll-saw blades.

Rip Cut Straight-line sawing in line with the grain. See Rip Cutting on pages 112 and 113.

Scroll Saw A power tool used for cutting wood, plastic, metal, and other material, usable for a wide range of cuts from simple outlines to intricate fretwork, inlays, intarsia, and marquetry.

Set A term used to describe the amount to which teeth are bent from the blade stock.

Skip-Tooth Blade A blade in which every other tooth is missing. This creates a gap equal to a whole tooth between the tooth points. See Blade Types on pages 73 to 76.

"Splitting the Line" By using a blade narrower than the marked line, it is possible to divide the line and leave a visual reference on each part of the separated workpieces. See What About the Saw Line? on pages 101 and 102.

S.P.M. (Strokes Per Minute) A term that refers to the speed of reciprocation of the scroll saw.

Stack-Cutting A technique used by scroll-sawyers in which several layers of material are cut at once.

Straight Fence An accessory fitted temporarily at a predetermined distance from the saw blade to help when cutting parallel strips. The workpiece is placed against the fence at the beginning of the cut and slid along it throughout the operation. See Straight Fence on pages 56 to 58.

Stroke Depth The distance the frame or arms on the scroll saw move from the top to the bottom of their stroke cycle.

Stroke Speed *See* s.p.m.

Surround A term that refers to a backing material to which a motif is added.

Template A pattern, cut from a thin durable material, of the exact size and shape of a part or component. See Cutting Templates for Curved Shapes on pages 120 to 123.

Throat Capacity The distance between the blade and the rear frame of the saw.

T.P.I (Teeth Per Inch) *See* pitch.

Universal General Numbering System
A grading system, used by some but not all manufacturers, as an attempt to create a standard specification of blade design. See Blade-Selection Guidelines on pages 67 to 71.

Wedge Inlay A motif, cut on a bevel from a panel and reinserted, like a wedge, into the aperture. Due to the angular cut, the motif protrudes slightly through the panel. See Intarsia With Wedge Inlays on pages 130 to 133.

METRIC EQUIVALENTS CHART

INCHES TO MILLEMETERS AND CENTIMETERS

MM— Millemeters   CM—Centimeters

Inches	MM	CM	Inches	CM	Inches	CM
⅛	3	0.3	9	22.9	30	76.2
¼	6	0.6	10	25.4	31	78.7
⅜	10	1.0	11	27.9	32	81.3
½	13	1.3	12	30.5	33	83.8
⅝	16	1.6	13	33.0	34	86.4
¾	19	1.9	14	35.6	35	88.9
⅞	22	2.2	15	38.1	36	91.4
1	25	2.5	16	40.6	37	94.0
1¼	32	3.2	17	43.2	38	96.5
1½	38	3.8	18	45.7	39	99.1
1¾	44	4.4	19	48.3	48	101.6
2	51	5.1	20	50.8	41	104.1
2½	64	6.4	21	53.3	42	106.7
3	76	7.6	22	55.9	43	109.2
3½	89	8.9	23	58.4	44	111.8
4	102	10.2	24	61.0	45	114.3
4½	114	11.4	25	63.5	46	116.8
5	127	12.7	25	66.0	47	119.4
6	152	15.2	27	68.6	48	121.9

Index

A

Abrading wood, accessories for, 45, 46, 47
Abrasive-coated rods, 76, 110
Abrasive drum, 42
Abrasive loops, 45, 46
Accessories
    for abrading wood, 45, 46, 47
    ancillary table, 63, 64-65
    awls for hole-boring, 53, 54-55
    blade-changing, 89-90
    blade container, 51, 52, 53
    circle-cutting jig, 61, 62, 63
    coolant dispenser, 51
    for cutting thin wood or metal, 49
    dust-extraction unit, 40, 41
    finger fence, 59-60
    flexible shaft, 41, 42
    foot switch, 39, 40
    geometrical protractor, 53
    hold-downs, 42, 43-44, 45
    machine stand, 47
    magnifier, 47, 48
    straight fence, 56-58
    vibration absorption mat, 48, 49
Adjusting blades
    angles other than 90 degrees, 92, 93
    longer, adjusting for, 94, 95
    right-angle, 91, 92
Aluminum, blades for cutting, 71

Ancillary table
    cutting small workpieces with a, 63-66, 118-119
    definition of, 149
Archimede's drills
    for blade-entry holes, 54, 65
    definition of, 149
Awl, 53, 54, 149

B

Bench scroll saw, 20, 21
Bevels, and blade angle, 92, 93
Blade-breakage device, 33, 34, 148, 149
Blade container, 51, 52, 53
Blade-entry holes
    for creating letters, 137
    determining and making, 54, 55
    for intarsia, 132, 136
Blade holders
    guidelines for, 78
    for pin-end blades, 79
    for pin- and plain-end blades, 80-81
    with pivot bar, 83
    quick-acting, 87-88
    split, 83
    stirrup-type, 83, 84
    for straight tracking, 96
    swiveling, 85-86
    V-shaped, 82

Blades
  and angle of deviation, 57, 58
  backs, rounding, 76
  bias, dealing with, 102
  burrs on, removing, 76
  cross-pins, modifying, 77
  holders for, 78, 79-90
  length of, 72
  longer, adjusting for, 94, 95
  section guidelines, 67-70, 71
  set, measuring, 73
  and "spin gap," 103, 104
  types of, 73-75, 76
  widths of, modifying, 77
Blade-tensioning devices
  on C-frame scroll saws, 26, 27
  guidelines for using, 27
  on parallel-arm scroll saws, 26, 27
Bodkin, user-made, 53, 54
Bone
  blades for cutting, 71
  cutting, 109, 110
Boulle, Andre Charles, 126
Boulle marquetry
  cutting techniques, 126-127, 128
  definition of, 149
Brass, blades for cutting, 71

C

Cabinet scraper, 140
Carborundum stone, for rounding blade backs,
    76
Cardboard, blades for cutting, 71
Ceramics, cutting, 110
C-frame scroll saw
  and blade-tensioning devices, 26, 27
  comparing to parallel-arm, 18-19
  definition of, 149
  parts of, 13, 14-15

Circles
  cutting technique, 114-114
  jig for cutting, 61-62, 63
Clamp-type blade holders, 87
Coolant dispenser, 51, 107, 108
Crosscutting, 111, 112, 149
Curves
  cutting technique, 113
  jig for cutting, 61-62, 63
Cutting speed, 21

D

Danish oil, 133
Depth of cut, 21, 22
Diamond scroll saw
  and blade holders, 94, 95
  and blade-tensioning devices, 26
  and flexible shaft, 41, 42
  and hold-down, 43, 44, 45
  and metal-cutting accessory, 49-50
  and rubber feet, 34
  and stroke depth, 22
  and stroke speed, 22
"Diamond"-coated files, 45
Drafting film for tracing templates, 121, 122,
    123
Dremel scroll saws
  and stroke speed and depth, 22
  and switches, 25
Drill set, 54, 55
Drive belts, maintaining, 37, 38
Dust blower
  definition of, 149
  maintenance of, 38
  types of, 29, 30
Dust-extraction unit, 40, 41, 149
Dust filters, 146, 147
Dust mask, 146, 147
Dust puffer, 149

E

Emery board and wood-abrasion, 45

F

Facemask, 146
Feed rate, 98, 149
Felt, blades for cutting, 71
Files, 45, 46
Fences
   finger, 59-69
   straight, 56-58
Finger fence
   definition of, 149
   using a, 59-60
"Flawless" marquetry, 128, 129, 130
Flexible drive. *See* flexible shaft
Flexible shaft, 41, 42, 150
Floor-model scroll saw, 20, 21
Foot switch
   as accessory, 39, 40
   definition of, 149
   with floor-model scroll saw, 20
   and hand placement, 101
Freestanding magnifiers, 48
Fretsaw. *See* Scroll Saw

G

Geometrical protractor
   to check blade angle, 92, 93
   description of, 53
Glass, cutting, 110
Goggles, 146
Golden Rule of scroll-sawing, 97
Guard
   for C-frame scroll saw, 15
   definition of, 150
   and safety techniques, 147
   types of, 32, 33
Gullet, 68

H

Hand placement, 98-99
Hardwoods, cutting characteristics of, 106
Hegner scroll saw
   and blade-tensioning devices, 26
   and dust blower, 30
   and hold-down, 42, 43
   and liquid coolant, 107
   and stroke depth, 22
Hold-downs
   as accessories, 42, 43-44
   definition of, 150
   types of, 30, 31, 32
Hole-boring, awls for, 53, 54-55
Hollow-form intarsia, 134-136, 150

I

Intarsia
   definition of, 150
   hollow-form, 134-136
   with wedge inlays, 130, 131-133
Internal-sawing, 124-125, 150
Ivory
   blades for cutting, 71
   cutting, 109, 110

J

Jewelers' blades, 74
Jigs
   ancillary table, 63-66
   blade-changing, 88, 89-90
   circle-cutting jig, 61-62, 63
   finger fence, 59-60
   straight fence, 56-58
Jigsaw. *See* Scroll Saw

K

Kerf
   definition of, 72, 150
   width of, 68

L

"Leaving the Line," 101, 102, 150

Letter guides, 137

Letters, creating, 137-140

Longer blades, adjusting for, 94, 95

M

Machine stand, 20, 214

Magnetic pads and blade storage, 53

Magnifier, 47, 48

Maintenance techniques, 35, 36-38, 145

Marquetry

    Boulle, 126, 127, 128

    definition of, 150

    "Flawless," 128, 129, 130, 150

Medium-density fiberboard

    blades for cutting, 71

    cutting characteristics of, 107

    definition of, 150

    practicing on-the-spot turns with, 102, 103, 104

Metal-cutting

    accessory for, 49, 50

    blades for, 74

    and coolant dispenser, 51

    techniques, 107, 108

Miters, and blade angle, 92

Motor housing and fans, maintaining, 37

Motor spindle bearings, lubricating, 36

N

Nameplate, creating a, 137-140

Non-wood material, cutting

    ceramics, glass, and stone, 110

    ivory and bone, 109, 110

    metal, 107

    plastics, 108, 108

    and Universal Generic Numbering system, 71

NVR switch, 150

O

On-off switches, 22, 24-25

On-the-spot turns

    definition of, 150

    description of, 102, 103, 104

    and internal-sawing, 125

P

Pantograph, 141, 142

Paper, blades for cutting, 71

Parallel-arm scroll saw

    and blade-tensioning devices, 26, 27

    comparing to C-frame scroll saw, 18-19

    parts of, 13,16-19, 21, 24, 25

Parallel curves, cutting, 59-60

Parallel strips, cutting, 56-58

Particleboard

    blades for cutting, 71

    cutting characteristics of, 107

    definition of, 150

    practicing on-the-spot turns with, 102, 103, 104

Patterns

    applying to wood, 143

    copying and transferring, 141, 142, 143

    templates as, 143, 144

    for wedge inlays, 131

Pierced-work. *See* Internal-Sawing

Pin-end blade

    blade holders for, 79-81

    to cut large workpieces, 77, 78, 116-117

    definition of, 150

    description of, 73

    modifying, 77, 78

Pitch, 68, 72, 150

Pitman arm

    for C-frame scroll saw, 14

    for parallel-arm scroll saw, 17

    and maintenance techniques, 37

and stroke depth, 23
Pivots, lubricating, 36
Plain-end blade
    blade holders for, 80-81
    definition of, 151
    description of, 73
    threading for intarsia, 132
Plastics,
    blades for cutting, 71
    cutting, 108, 109
Plucking a blade, 27
Plywood
    blades for cutting, 71
    used for nameplate, 139
Poolewood scroll saws
    and blade-tensioning devices, 26
    and rubber feet, 34
    and switches, 25
Pouncing wheel, 173, 174

Q

Quick-acting blade holders
    and creating letters, 138
    description of, 87, 88

R

Reverse-tooth blade
    definition of, 151
    description of, 75
    with a plain end, 73
Rexon scroll saws, switches on, 22, 25
Right-angle blade adjustment, 91, 92
Rip cut, 112, 113, 151
Rocker switches, 25
Rounding blade backs, 76
Rubber, blades for cutting, 71
Rubber feet, 34

S

Safety glasses, 146

Safety procedures, 145-145-148
"Sapphire"-coated files, 45
Saw line, 101, 102
Scroll saw
    accessories, 39-66
    clamping to workbench, 148
    components of, maintaining, 35, 36-38
    definition of, 151
    evolution of, 11
    and safety factors, 12
    standard features, 21-34, 35
    types of, 13-20, 21
Sears Craftsman scroll saws
    and blade-tensioning devices, 26
    and maintenance techniques, 36, 37
    and switches, 25
Set, 71, 151
Skip-tooth blades, 74, 75, 151
Small pieces, cutting, 63, 64-66, 118-119
Softwoods, cutting characteristics of, 106
Spin gap, 103, 104
Spiral blades,
    description of, 75, 76
    sawing with, 137-140
Splitting the line, 102, 151
S.P.M., 151
Spray-on adhesive, 131
Stack-cutting, 126, 151
Steel
    blades for cutting, 71
    cutting, 108
Steering techniques
    blade bias, 102
    on-the-spot turns, 101, 102, 103
    saw line, 101, 102
Stirrup-type blade holders, 83-84
Stone, cutting, 110
"Stop screw," 93
Storage box, 33

Straight fence
  definition of, 151
  using a, 56-58
Straight tracking, 94, 95, 96
Stroke depth
  changing, 23
  definition of, 22, 151
  verifying, 23
Stroke length, 21
Stroke speed
  definition of, 151
  description of, 22
  and Golden Rule of scroll-sawing, 97
Surround, definition of, 151
Switches, 22, 24-25
Swiveling blade holders, 85-86

T

Table inserts
  description of, 34, 35
  removing, 84
Templates
  for curved shapes, 120-123
  definition of, 151
  as patterns, 143, 144
Thickness of blade, 68
Thimbles and scroll-sawing, 119
Throat capacity, 21, 151
Throat depth, cutting workpieces longer than, 77, 78
Tool-Bridge, 49-50, 107

Tooth depth, 68
T.P.I., definition of, 151

U

Universal Generic Numbering system
  and the cutting of different materials, 71
  definition of, 151
  and the selection of scroll-saw blades, 67-69

V

Veneer, stacking-cutting, 126, 127, 128
Vibration absorption mat, 48
V-shaped blade holders, 82

W

"Walking" hand technique, 100, 101
Wedge inlays
  definition of, 151
  intarsia with, 130, 131-133
Width of blade,
  definition of, 68
  measuring, 54
Wood
  choosing, 105, 106, 107
  cutting thick, 74
Wood-cutting blades, 73, 74
Workpieces
  large, cutting, 116-117
  longer than throat depth, 77, 78, 86
  small, cutting, 63-66, 118-119
  thick, cutting, 145
Worktable tilt, 28, 29